For Mojo, Soko,
Phantom, Heyoka and Sequoia

Other books by the author:

Living with Wolfdogs

Wolfdogs A-Z: Behavior, Training & More

It's Not the Dogs, It's the People! A Dog Trainer's Guide to Training Humans (also available on audio CD)

One on One: A Dog Trainer's Guide to Private Lessons

Help for Your Fearful Dog

Getting a Grip on Aggression Cases

Energy Healing for Dogs

So You Want to be a Dog Trainer

Step-by-Step Advice from a Professional

Nicole Wilde, CPDT

So You Want To Be A Dog Trainer
by Nicole Wilde

Published by:
Phantom Publishing
P.O. Box 2814
Santa Clarita, CA 91386

Second Edition

ISBN 978-0-9667726-8-5

Library of Congress Control Number: 2006902372

Cover photo: Tia Torres
All other photos by the author.

ACKNOWLEDGEMENTS

I would like to thank:

Dr. Ian Dunbar for his support, friendship and encouragement. Ian, without you I never would have published the first book, never mind the next five.

Laura Bourhenne for her generosity, feedback and uncanny ability to catch those errors no one else does.

Mychelle and Jake Blake for allowing me to use their lovely dogs as head halter/collar models.

Thanks as always to my wonderful husband C.C., who not only reads each manuscript, but provides encouragement, support, and puts up with an awful lot of "dog stuff." I really did marry the best guy in the world.

Last but never least, I am deeply grateful to Mojo, Soko, Phantom, Heyoka, Sequoia, and the countless dogs and wolves who have shared love, laughter and lessons over the years. They will always be my best and most beloved teachers.

☼ Table of Contents ☼

Group Classes

Foreword

It is somewhat unusual for the second edition of a book to be released just five years after its initial printing. In this case, the need for an updated version was created by an influx of new and exciting resources for dog trainers. There are now better training tools and products, more educational opportunities, and cost-effective ways to advertise your business. It would be a shame not to put that information at your fingertips!

One of the first steps in the process of becoming a dog trainer is to get educated about canine cognition and behavior. Since the first printing of this book, exciting new educational opportunities have emerged. Some involve classes that must be attended in person. Others offer the convenience of learning from home, either in the form of online classes, or through telecourses or webinars—seminars that are presented via telephone or online. The *Resources* section of this book has been expanded to include a number of organizations and educational opportunities that can benefit aspiring and established trainers alike.

The section on how to advertise your business has been updated as well. Searching for goods and services on the internet has become so commonplace that "Google" is now a commonly accepted verb. Having an effective website, and knowing how to drive prospective clients to that site, is a necessity in today's competitive business climate. Included are tips and resources for creating a website and establishing a presence.

Also included in this edition are new tools and products that can help you to help your clients' dogs with a variety of training and behavior issues.

You have chosen a very exciting time to become a dog trainer!

Introduction

There are countless instructional books and DVDs on the market about dog training. Most are geared toward pet owners, and focus on training techniques and solving common behavior problems. But what if your goal is not simply to train your own dog, but to become a professional dog trainer? Where can you turn for information on getting an education, creating a business, dealing with clients, and all of the countless details that are involved in the profession? There certainly doesn't seem to be a glut of information available. Of course, what would be of real value would be to have a friend who has been in the business for years, and is willing to give you the inside scoop; someone who would let you in on trade secrets, offer motivation and share great ideas. ...Think of me as that friend.

We'll take it slowly, step by step. First, we'll consider factors that will help you to decide whether a dog training career is truly something you want to pursue. Then we'll discuss various types of training, how to go about getting an education (which, by the way, doesn't necessarily mean going back to school), the nuts and bolts of setting up your business, dealing with clients, and much more. (All of this, and you don't even have to buy me dinner!)

Allow me to share my own first experience with dog training. I was fourteen, and my mother had registered me and my Schipperke mix Skippy (creative name, I know) for a group obedience class. I was secretly thrilled. Becoming a dog trainer was a fantasy I had harbored but could never admit to my parents. In my family, you were expected to finish school and get the sort of job you could "fall back on," something stable and sensible, such as being a teacher. Suffice it to say that aspiring to become a dog trainer was not a notion that would have been well received. I couldn't wait for the class to begin.

The first day of class was filled with anxious dogs and nervous owners. We watched as the instructor explained and demonstrated each exercise. She seemed a nice enough woman, but appeared to believe that a certain amount of physical force was necessary in order to teach dogs. For example, to teach a dog to lie down, she would bring her foot down forcefully on the leash, very close to the dog's neck; this would cause the dog's head to hit the ground, and the body would follow. Although I was apprehensive about using some of these techniques that were so different than what I had imagined, I dutifully tried each one with Skippy. Although she was an extremely intelligent dog, Skippy did not look as though she was having fun.

As the dogs learned new skills, the owners were taught how to correct them if they did not comply. We learned how to jerk and release the metal choke chains the dogs wore around their necks, with enough force that they would "understand they had no choice." Although I was young and inexperienced, I could see that my dog was upset; so was I. Some of the other dogs and owners seemed stressed as well. Some dogs were getting more and more agitated and less able to concentrate. As their owners became more frustrated, the jerking became more forceful. I wanted to cry. Never in my fantasies had dog training been like this! Though we completed the course, I was crushed. I knew I could never bring myself to do those things to dogs, so how could I ever hope to become a dog trainer?

Fast forward thirty years. Great news! Dog training has changed in remarkable ways. Thanks to pioneers like Dr. Ian Dunbar, Karen Pryor, Jean Donaldson and others, more and more trainers are discovering the joy and the power of positive training. Rather than being physically coerced into learning, dogs are set up to succeed by making learning easy. It's just like teaching children; we take it one step at a time, and use patience, consistency and kindness. When a dog performs an exercise correctly, he is rewarded. Reward-based training is not only effective, but is enjoyable for both dogs and owners.

You might be wondering how I got involved in a career in dog training, after I had given up on it years ago. The answer is, indirectly. I was volunteering with an organization in southern California that rescues wolves and wolfdogs (wolf-dog mixes). In addition to tending to the daily care and socialization of the sanctuary's residents, I often visited the homes of wolfdog owners who needed assistance. Many were at the point of being forced to give up their beloved pets if something did not change. I assisted owners in building proper enclosures, and to the extent that I could, helped with training and behavior issues. I never considered charging for my services, and I learned a lot through the hands-on experience.

Over the next ten years, while working full-time, I volunteered at a city shelter where I interacted with dogs of various breeds and temperaments, co-ran the rescue center, and eventually, began training dogs for the general public for a fee. I found that while training wolves and wolfdogs can be difficult, training domestic dogs is much easier—although training the owners can sometimes be a challenge. I finally made the leap to training dogs as a full-time business. I now work daily with a variety of wonderful dogs, meet interesting people, set my own hours, and enjoy a healthy income. Spending time with dogs, teaching dogs and people new skills, and helping to modify the behavior of dogs who might otherwise lose their homes is incredibly fulfilling. And to think, you actually get paid for this!

Now, you might be thinking that while this all sounds wonderful, you have some personal roadblock to pursuing dog training as a career. Perhaps you lack experience with dogs; maybe you believe you are too old to start a new career; or, perhaps you find dealing with people challenging. Whatever your concern, set it aside. Armed with the information in this book and the willingness to put in the necessary time and effort, you *can* become a dog trainer. *Let's get started!*

Why Do You Want
to Train Dogs?

I love dogs. Maybe you do too, and that's why you want to become a trainer. Actually, that's the reason a lot of people get into this business. Others get involved because they not only like dogs, but also enjoy working with people. There is a lot of "people training" involved in the profession, in the form of conveying information, coaching, and offering support and encouragement. The best trainers enjoy and excel at working with both dogs and people. A third incentive for becoming a dog trainer is financial gain. Let's examine each of these motivations.

"I Love Dogs!"

If you are a dog lover, training can be extremely fulfilling on an emotional level. It is wonderful to see a dog who was formerly kept outdoors now living indoors as part of the family because he's better behaved, thanks to your efforts. I cannot begin to describe the joy I feel when a client says, "We were so close to giving our dog up. Thank you for helping us to keep him. We really love him." How's *that* for job satisfaction? It's a real thrill too to get to the root of a dog's behavior issue, design a program to address it, and see progress being made. Watching a dog who was previously frightened of people accept petting and treats from strangers is heartwarming. Watching a dog who had been reactive toward other dogs romp and play with them is amazing. And seeing the harmony that exists between a dog and its family, knowing you helped to create it, is priceless.

While having a love of and compassion for canines is conducive to being a great trainer, it can also make your job difficult at times. You will inevitably visit homes where the dog is kept in less than ideal conditions, or is even mistreated.

If you deal with aggressive dogs, there will be cases where an owner, perhaps with your input, makes the decision to euthanize the dog. Will those cases affect you to the point that you lose sleep, or become depressed or angry? Those reactions are certainly understandable. But consider carefully, and be honest with yourself. Would that same love of dogs that makes you want to be a trainer cause too much wear and tear on your emotional well-being? There is a lot of responsibility involved in helping to make life and death decisions, and there surely will be rare cases where despite your best efforts, the situation is just not salvageable. Would you blame yourself if that happened, or know that you did your best under the circumstances?

Happily, the majority of training cases do not involve such dire decisions, and if you decide not to take on advanced behavior issues such as aggression, you can most likely avoid those situations. Still, will your love of dogs allow you to assess situations objectively and give constructive advice rather than blurting out comments like, "Of course he's destroying things, he's stuck in the yard all day and bored to tears!" (*That* scenario, unfortunately, is not at *all* uncommon.) Trust me, there are times when we all want to do the latter, and doing the former takes self-control—but it's necessary. You owe it to yourself to think realistically about whether you can deal with the emotional aspects of the profession. For the most part, though, there are vastly more positive outcomes than negative, and much that is emotionally rewarding.

"I'm a People Person"

Some people get into dog training because they enjoy working with and helping people. Are you a "people person?" Consider very carefully, because *at least half of dog training is really about training the owners*. This is a customer service business where you will deal with all types of people. Some will be absolutely wonderful, some ignorant, and a few, downright unpleasant. You will definitely need "people skills" as well as dog training skills to be a good, effective trainer. Having a background in psychology or social work can help, but is not necessary; what *is* necessary is having empathy for people, and treating them with kindness and patience. Dog owners don't want to hear that they're doing it all wrong, no matter how badly they're doing it. You must develop a talent for finding the good and praising it in people, just as you would with dogs. When a client just doesn't "get" what you are trying to explain, and fumbles an exercise over and over, what will you do? Will you treat it as a training problem, and patiently break the task into smaller, more manageable steps in order to help your client succeed? Or will you become frustrated and lose your patience?

You will find yourself in homes with screaming, out-of-control children (my toughest personal challenge), and clients who take phone calls and allow other interruptions during your sessions. Some people will argue with everything you say, while others will argue with their spouses or children in front of you. I have found myself in situations where I'd swear I was watching that old television show *Family Feud*. It was all I could do not to shout out, "Good answer! Good answer!" Take a deep breath and ask yourself whether those types of situations are something you realistically can or want to deal with.

Keep in mind that I am laying out the less appealing scenarios so you can take everything into consideration. The fact is, most people you will work with will be friendly and truly want what's best for their dogs. After all, that's why they called a trainer in the first place. Most will be willing to listen, and will appreciate your assistance. Many will tell you how much your training has helped. It won't hurt your ego, either, when you get a dog to behave well and the client, amazed, asks when you can move in with them. (Nothing wrong with a little positive reinforcement for the trainer!) I have had so many wonderful clients over the years who I never would have had the opportunity to meet otherwise. I have become friends with some and have stayed in touch with others, just because they and their dogs were so lovely. If you enjoy interacting with people and can be a patient teacher, this career may just be for you.

Ka-Ching!

Now we come to the part you may be unsure about—finances. Can you really make a decent living as a dog trainer? The answer is yes. Will you make a fortune? Probably not, especially at the beginning. Like any other business, it can be tough when you are just starting out. It takes most businesses an average of a year for word of mouth to start spreading. Dog training is no exception. It also normally takes approximately three years for a small business to begin turning a profit. In dog training, unless you have overhead to pay on a training facility, you can start to make a profit almost immediately, but it will still take time to build your business. You will incur initial expenses such as liability insurance, training equipment, and advertising; but if you market yourself well, do a good job, and people like you, you are on your way.

A safe way to ease into dog training is to work at a full-time or part-time job while training on the side. As your business builds, you can gradually switch over to training full-time. Some people opt to train part-time on a permanent basis. That's one of the great things about this career—you get to make your own schedule.

What type of training you choose to do will largely determine your income. Group classes have been called the "bread and butter" of the business. It is true that group classes afford a more steady income than the hit-and-miss scheduling of private, one-on-one sessions. Clients normally sign up for an average of eight group lessons in advance, which ensures a guaranteed weekly income over that period. Some trainers do nothing but group classes, love what they do, and earn a good living. In the next chapter we will discuss various types of group classes you might want to offer.

Many trainers earn a substantial income doing only private, in-home training. Private trainers teach obedience skills, and also address common behavior issues such as jumping on visitors, housebreaking, and inappropriate chewing. Once word of mouth gets around and your business becomes established, you could end up doing anywhere from five to twenty in-home appointments a week. The down side of in-home sessions is cancellations, and the potential lack of steady scheduling during slow times such as holidays and vacation periods.

An option you might not have considered is board-and-train. That means you train the client's dog at your own home or kennel (or a boarding kennel with which you have an arrangement) for an agreed-upon length of time. Board-and-train can be quite profitable, and gives you valuable one-on-one time with the dog. Some trainers do board-and-train and also offer boarding without training. If you have the facilities and proper licensing, either option is an excellent way to enhance your training income.

Regardless of which type or types of training you do, there will always be peaks and lulls throughout the year. Many people vacation in the summer when the kids are off school; business may be slow during that time. It is likely to be sporadic during and closely following the holiday season, but may well pick up a month or two later when all those cute holiday gift-pups start to display typical puppy behavior problems.

Climate may seem an odd thing to consider, but depending on where you live and what type of training you do, the weather can affect your business. I live in southern California. Because of the mild climate, outdoor classes are held almost year-round. In New York, where I am originally from, not many people want to train in the rain and snow, so mid-winters are a slow time for group classes, unless they are held indoors.

Consider the climate in which you live. Will it literally "put a damper" on your income? If you plan on offering group classes only, and having a steady income year-round is crucial, consider holding on to that part-time job even after your business is established, or taking temporary jobs during slow periods. That way, when business is slow you will still have a way to pay the bills.

Next, we'll discuss the various types of training in more depth.

What Type of Training Will You Do?

Although this book focuses on only one aspect of dog training—training pet dogs—there are still a variety of ways to provide that service. Following are a few of the most common.

Obedience Training

Some trainers choose to offer obedience instruction only, as opposed to dealing with behavior issues as well; that can be a good choice for the beginning trainer. Obedience skills may be taught in a group class setting, or privately in clients' homes.

Private lessons are normally done with the owner present; after all, you really are training the owner to train the dog. But some trainers set up a schedule where they work with dogs alone, usually a few times a week. Those visits are followed up by periodic sessions with the client to show the behaviors the dog has learned, and to teach the owner how to get the dog to perform those behaviors. This type of regimen is convenient for owners who are too busy to do regular training and practice sessions themselves. On the other hand, sessions that are always done with the owner present have the advantage of providing the owner with more one-on-one instruction and feedback.

Group Classes

If you choose to teach group obedience classes, you will have some decisions to make. First, where will your classes be held? If you are the employee of a chain pet supply store or other business that offers training, space will be provided for you. If not, you could offer classes through local pet supply stores or veterinary clinics. In those cases, classes are normally held in the parking lot, or inside, if space allows. Sign-up sheets are usually displayed on-site to lure potential clients.

Some trainers lease space through their local Parks and Recreation Department. "Parks and Rec" classes have the advantage of a nice park setting, and offer the opportunity for your classes to be seen by bystanders, who might then sign up themselves. Many parks departments will even promote the classes for you. However, almost all will take a percentage of your profits, which will affect how many dogs you must have in class to make it financially worthwhile.

Other potential places to hold classes include church or store parking lots, school gymnasiums or auditoriums, and veterans halls. Consider the climate where you live, and whether the weather will permit you to train outdoors year-round. If not, an indoor facility might be more advantageous. You could even eventually opt to lease a space to create your own training facility.

Another group class consideration is size. Some chain pet supply stores offer classes that enroll up to twenty dogs, with only one instructor. However, unless you have assistants, you are better off keeping your classes small. A good rule of thumb is to have a maximum of six dogs per instructor. That way you can monitor the dogs' behavior and give everyone the quality, hands-on attention they deserve. People really appreciate that!

You could also offer "semi-private group classes" limited to, say, four dogs. I have not seen this type of class advertised much, but when I offered them, the response was positive. Semi-private groups offer an alternative to those who cannot or do not want to pay for in-home, one-on-one visits, but do not want a large, impersonal group, either. And, that exclusive, "semi-private" label really appeals to certain people.

You will also have to decide what level of obedience you will offer. Some trainers, especially when they are first starting out, offer basic obedience and nothing more. That's fine! The majority of dog owners would benefit greatly from training their dogs in the basics, even if they never went further. Of course, you could also offer intermediate and advanced classes. For more in-depth considerations regarding group classes, see Chapter 18, *Group Class Considerations*.

Puppy Kindergarten

A fun and important type of group class you might want to offer is Puppy Kindergarten. The emphasis in these classes is on socialization, along with common puppy issues such as nipping, chewing, jumping up and housebreaking. Owners are often relieved to find that their pup is not the only one having those problems!

Puppy classes should include handling and restraint exercises, which will make future groomer and vet visits easier and help the puppy/owner bond. Interactive food/treat dispensers (I call these "puppy pacifiers") such as the Kong® should be shown and explained (see Chapter 15, *Your Toolbox*). Students should be taught to manage the home environment and supervise so their pups don't get into trouble in the first place. In-class socialization should include introducing pups to all sorts of unfamiliar things including strange sounds, different types of surfaces to walk on, and things that can sometimes frighten dogs such as people wearing hats and sunglasses. Most puppy classes also include an introduction to basic obedience. Those pups are not too young to learn!

Traditional puppy classes start at four months of age. That's because sixteen weeks is the age at which the rabies vaccination is given, along with the last of the series of puppy vaccinations. Many veterinarians feel it is unsafe to expose puppies to other dogs before the vaccination series is complete. However, the optimum window of socialization in dogs is between four and twelve weeks of age. It's not that a puppy can't be socialized after that; but if a pup is exposed to new things (including other dogs and people) during that four-to-twelve-week period, he is much more likely to accept them, and have less of a fearful reaction to those things in the future.

Many trainers feel that as long as pups are healthy and have had at least two or three rounds of vaccinations, they are eligible for puppy class. Naturally, you will want to make sure the area you teach in is free of potential disease-causing germs. If your class is held at a veterinary clinic, make sure the floors are thoroughly disinfected before class. Do not hold puppy classes at a public park, since there would be a risk of the pups contracting diseases such as parvo or distemper from sick dogs who had been there before.

If you choose to accept very young pups into class, you might want to bring the maximum age down a bit so that you don't end up with three-month-olds being overwhelmed by six-month-olds in play. For more in-depth information on puppy classes, see Chapter 21, *Puppy Kindergarten*.

Other types of group classes you could offer include trick training (see *Resources*), clicker training (more on that later), one-topic classes (for example, a four-week session on leashwork only), and "growl" classes for dog-aggressive dogs. *Growl classes should never be taught by novice trainers*, but are something you might want to consider later on, as you gain confidence and experience in dealing with aggressive behavior.

In-Home Training

Some trainers prefer to do in-home, private training only. They screen clients carefully by phone, then go to their homes to train. If you are lucky enough to have your own office or facility, private clients can come to you. A private trainer might also accompany clients to temperament-test potential adoptees, to ensure a good match.

In-home training constitutes the majority of my own practice, and I enjoy it immensely. So much progress can be made when you are able to give your full attention to an individual dog/owner team. Unfortunately, that level of personal engagement can be a double-edged sword. On one hand, it is both fascinating and rewarding to figure out what is at the root of a behavior problem, observe dog/owner interactions, design behavior modification programs, and see progress being made. On the other hand, when you have a difficult client (usually the person, not the dog), there you are—one-on-one. While having good people skills is important in a group setting, it is crucial in private training. Fortunately, the majority of dog owners are a pleasure to work with. (For help in dealing with those who are not, see the *Resources* section for books, including my own *It's Not the Dogs, It's the People!*)

While some clients will call you to their homes for obedience training only, the problem will sometimes be a behavior issue. A "behavior issue" can be anything from jumping on the kids, to darting out the front door, to separation anxiety (the dog becoming stressed when left alone), or even biting people. There are more behavior issues than I could possibly list, and variations on each one. You will get a feel for which issues you are comfortable working with as you go; just don't take on any behavior issue until you feel confident and knowledgable enough to do a good job for the client.

The first few years I trained, I did not work with aggressive dogs at all. If I got aggression calls, I referred them to another trainer; I suggest you do the same. There is absolutely nothing wrong with referring clients to another trainer who has more expertise and experience with a particular issue—in fact, it's the right thing to do, for everybody's sake. I now regularly work with dog-aggressive and people-aggressive dogs, but if an extreme case comes along, I might still confer with or even refer to a veterinary behaviorist who specializes in aggression.

If you are going to work with dog-dog aggression issues, consider whether you have a dog of your own who does not become reactive when other dogs do. It is much easier to desensitize dog-aggressive dogs to being around others if your own dog is not reactive. Do you own or have access to a dog with a "bomb-proof" temperament? If not, you can still work with dog-aggressive dogs but it will be more challenging, as you will have to depend on working with dogs you encounter randomly in public from the start, as opposed to working the client's dog up to that level.

How many sessions does in-home training take? It depends. A simple behavior issue such as housebreaking will probably merit only one visit. By that I do not mean that you come in, wave a magic wand, and *poof!* the client's dog will never again have a potty accident. But in one session, you should be able to set up a management and housebreaking program the client understands and is able to carry out without further visits. Simple behavior issues such as stealing items from countertops, darting out the front door, and jumping on visitors may take a few sessions. More serious behavior issues, such as those involving fear and aggression, will take longer. The number of sessions needed will depend on the individual dog, how long the behavior has been going on, the severity of the issue, and the level of owner commitment.

You might, as many trainers do, decide to sell "packages" of sessions. For example, if you see that a behavior issue will require more than a few visits, you could have the client pay you in advance for four, six, or more sessions. This is common practice with in-home clients who want a full obedience course. The package deal is not only financially advantageous to you as a trainer, but also motivates clients to stick with the program.

If you decide to offer package deals, have a contract prepared that outlines the terms of your arrangement. It is also a good idea to include a clause that stipulates a date by which the sessions must be completed. Otherwise, you could end up with a client who constantly postpones appointments, which would affect the program's continuity. (See *The Dog Trainer's Business Kit* CD-ROM in the *Resources* section for comprehensive, easy-to-use contracts.)

Board-and-Train

You might decide that rather than holding group classes or doing in-home training, you prefer to board and train dogs in your own home. Should you choose this option, your first job is to research the business and zoning laws in your area. A board and train arrangement may require a business license, and possibly a kennel license as well. Check with your local City Clerk's office for legalities and requirements.

Another important board-and-train consideration is how many dogs you can accommodate, and how well you are set up to manage them. For example, some dogs will not get along well with others. If you plan to board more than one trainee at a time, will you be able to keep them separated? Liability goes hand in hand with boarding; you are completely responsible for the welfare of the dogs in your care.

On the positive side, board and train is a great way to provide quality training time. Sometimes removing a dog from its home environment offers a better chance to work through certain issues, especially ones in which owners are unwitting contributers. It is rewarding to see the joy on an owner's face when you show off how much progress their four-footed darling has made. Board and train can also be very satisfying on a financial level.

Other Options

Other training options include offering instruction at an established boarding facility, or at a shelter where your training will help the dogs to get adopted.

All of the options mentioned so far presume that you are a one-person business. If you don't want to jump in with both feet, there are alternatives, such as working for a company where you would be trained to teach group classes and possibly to do in-home training. In addition to local organizations, two national chains, PetSmart and PETCO, each have their own programs to educate and employ new trainers.

Don't let these considerations overwhelm you. You don't have to make any decisions right now; besides, you might, like so many trainers, start out doing one thing and naturally move into another.

Next, we'll discuss ways to begin or enhance your dog training education.

3

Getting an Education

Training has Changed

Dog training has changed a lot over the last thirty years. Traditional obedience training often involved physical force and coercion, and was not always pleasant for dogs or people. More and more trainers are now using fun, humane methods like lure-reward and clicker training. Lure-reward training uses food treats to lure dogs into position, and to reward them. For example, to lure a dog from a sit into a down, a treat is held to the dog's nose, and then moved in a straight line down to the ground. The dog follows the treat until he is lying down; there is no physical coercion involved. The dog is then given the treat as a reward.

Clicker training has been used with marine mammals and exotics for many years, and is a fun and effective way to train dogs. A small device called a clicker is used to mark the exact moment a dog is performing a behavior correctly. The click is then followed by a treat. Dogs learn quickly that a click equals a treat, so they begin to try to figure out what to do to earn the click. The method teaches dogs to think for themselves. It is very effective for teaching obedience skills and modifying behavior problems, and is an excellent method for teaching tricks. The *Resource* section includes books that explain clicker training in depth.

Choice of Training Techniques

In seeking out education and experience, it is important to be aware that a wide variety of training techniques and styles exist. Some trainers consider themselves "totally positive trainers," because they do not use corrections at all. Others use verbal corrections and mild aversives such as squirt bottles, but eschew tools such as choke chains or shock collars (also called electronic collars, or e-collars). Some trainers teach dogs by using lure-reward and other positive methods, then use corrections for non-compliance. Others bypass treats altogether, preferring to use only praise and corrections. Some trainers who use both positive reinforcement and corrections refer to themselves as "balanced trainers." Even within these categories there are variations; what constitutes a "correction," for example, can vary from trainer to trainer, and also depends on the particular situation. And lastly, there are trainers who use excessive physical force—some to correct a dog who is not complying with a request, some to teach new skills, and some, to do both. The use of excessive force should not be considered training, but abuse.

In researching any school or individual offering training, be sure to ask about techniques, and watch how the dogs are trained. Choose a teacher with whose methods you feel comfortable. On your journey to becoming a professional trainer, you will cross paths with trainers from all philosophies. Keep in mind that you can learn something from everyone, even if it is only to decide what you *don't* want to incorporate into your own training.

Association of Pet Dog Trainers (APDT)

One of the best things you can do in your quest for knowledge is to join the Association of Pet Dog Trainers (APDT). Founded by Dr. Ian Dunbar, a pioneer in positive training methods, the organization focuses on promoting dog-friendly training techniques and the ongoing education of its members. You need not be a professional trainer to join. An annual membership entitles you to the organization's monthly magazine *The Chronicle of the Dog*, discounts on conferences, and membership in the online discussion list. *The Chronicle* alone is worth it! It is filled with news about the organization and its members, fascinating training articles and columns, tips and tricks on solving behavior issues, information about new products and upcoming seminars, and more.

The APDT internet discussion list is an amazing resource as well. New trainers can ask questions about anything from training techniques to ethical dilemmas with clients, and everything in-between. Many experienced trainers participate and are generous with their advice. Trainers at all levels share their experiences and tips on common behavior issues, post case histories, and receive feedback and suggestions. Support and encouragement is offered to those who need it, and information is shared about products and upcoming seminars.

Speaking of seminars, the APDT Annual Educational Conference is not to be missed! Held in a different part of the United States each year, this five-day extravaganza immerses trainers in seminars and workshops taught by some of the world's top trainers. It affords trainers the opportunity to meet and learn from some of the folks whose books they've been reading, and to network with other trainers from around the world. The conference also hosts a large trade show where you can check out the latest training equipment, get bargains on all manner of dog-related products, and attend live demonstrations throughout the day.

I can tell you first-hand that no matter what your level of knowledge, from novice to experienced, the APDT will be an incredible help to you. I credit the organization's seminars, internet list, newsletters and networking with contributing immensely to my own education. And although I now speak at their conferences, my education through the organization continues. The APDT is the world's largest organization for dog trainers for good reason. (See *Resources* for contact information.)

Schools, Academies, and Courses

As mentioned, there is no degree necessary to become a dog trainer. You might, however, wish to pursue an academic course in order to expand your knowledge and to increase your credibility. Degrees that would be helpful in working with dogs include those in Applied Psychology, Ethology and Zoology, and Applied Animal Behavior. Most require undergraduate work in areas such as biology and other sciences. You could go on to get a Masters and even a Ph.D.—but keep in mind that you can still be a fantastic dog trainer without holding a single degree.

Most traditional schools expect you to attend in person, complete the coursework, and accumulate a certain amount of hands-on experience. Fortunately, there are now new and exciting opportunities for both on-site and distance learning. Following are some excellent choices.

San Francisco SPCA

The San Francisco SPCA, located in northern California, offers on-site courses on dog training and behavior counseling using positive reinforcement-based methods. The academy's main instructors are renowned trainer/author Jean Donaldson, and Janis Bradley, a clicker trainer and educator with 20 years experience in curriculum design and counseling. Some of the top names in the dog training field serve as guest lecturers. The organization's web site calls the CTC (Certificate in Training and Counseling) program, "a six-week, full-time course designed to provide a thorough, well-rounded education in pet dog training and behavior counseling. The curriculum combines lecture, video, demonstration and round-table discussion with hands-on training as well as rehearsal of instructing and interviewing skills." (There is a six-day advanced course as well.) Students work with shelter dogs, complete homework assignments, and get lots of personal feedback. If you can spare the expense and the six weeks away from home, and meet the enrollment requirements, this might be the school for you. For contact information for the SF SPCA as well as for all of the following educational organizations mentioned in this section, see the *Resources* section.

Marin Humane Society

Also located in northern California, the Marin Humane Society offers 10-week courses for those who wish to become professional trainers, as well as those who are simply interested in learning more about training and behavior. The curriculum includes ethology, breed characteristics, social and learning theory, behavioral problems and behavior modification techniques, handling, conducting consulations, and much more. The Director of Training is Trish King, author, trainer and popular seminar presenter.

Moorpark College

Another excellent opportunity exists to gain training skills, not with dogs, but with exotic animals. Moorpark College, located in southern California, offers a unique opportunity for students to work with exotic animals ranging from marmosets to elephants, alligators to big cats. Students come from all over the world to work with the 150 animals in the EATM (Exotic

Animal Training and Management) program. Students are expected to work many nights and weekends; the program is very intense. Although dogs are not part of the program, working with exotics will give you invaluable training in operant conditioning and make you a much better dog trainer. You could even earn an Associate in Science degree.

Peacable Paws, located in Maryland, is headed by trainer/author Pat Miller. The internships and apprenticeships include both theory and hands-on positive training.

Sue Sternberg is an author/trainer/lecturer who specializes in working with shelter dogs. At Rondout Valley Kennels in Accord, New York, Sue offers short courses for trainers that include all aspects of canine behavior and training.

Dogs of Course offers five-day training courses for instructors, as well as workshops and seminars around the country.

Legacy Canine Behavior and Training, headed by author/trainer and popular seminar speaker Terry Ryan, hosts an annual Instructor's Course in Sequim, Washington and hosts other seminars as well.

Suzanne Clothier, a popular seminar presenter, author, and trainer, offers annual workshops for trainers based on her Relationship Centered Training™ at her upstate New York facility.

In addition to courses and workshops, there are plenty of one-day and weekend seminars available. An excellent way to find out about current seminars and workshops in your area is to log on to the Dog Seminars Directory website at www.dogseminarsdirectory.com. Run by trainer Caryl Wolff, the site allows for searches by subject, location, speaker, or date.

Other Training Academies

You have probably seen ads in national magazines, on the internet, and elsewhere for dog training schools and academies. When researching any potential educational facility, keep in mind that a good curriculum should include an overview of training, theory, breed characteristics, genetics, social development, behavior issues, and business considerations. It should also offer plenty of hands-on experience with a variety of dogs. Ask for contact information for students who have attended the school, and get their feedback. Ask whether you can observe a class where students are training dogs. There is a wide variety of techniques used in training schools, ranging from those that are dog-friendly to those that are excessively harsh. If there is anything you are not comfortable with, don't assume the instructors are right in their methodology just because they have more experience. They might simply be using methods that do not interest you. Keep looking until you find the right fit.

Distance Learning

Companion Animal Sciences Institute (CASI)

For those who cannot spare the time away from home, online education offers the perfect option. The Companion Animal Sciences Insitute (formerly Cynology College), a well-respected distance education school, provides challenging, in-depth certificate courses and diploma programs. Although the school is distance-oriented, the courses make use of hands-on and practical assignments, and there are optional practicum and supervised programs as well.

Enrollment automatically gives students the benefit of participating in the Virtual Classroom, an online venue where students can discuss and ask questions about assignments and behavioral issues, and receive help with actual cases. Students can also network virtually with live guest speakers, including world-renowned trainers, behaviorists, and scientists.

American College of Applied Science (ACAS)

Based in Florida, ACAS offers the first Bachelor of Science degree in Companion Animal Science in the United States. The objective of this online degree program is to prepare individuals to work in the field of animal science and care, with a special emphasis on domesticated companion animals. Study topics include biology, psychology, animal anatomy/physiology, learning and behavior, nutrition, and more. The program typically takes two to three years to complete. For those who wish to pursue an advanced degree, a Masters Degree in Companion Animal Behavior Counseling is offered. The school also offers a Dog Training and Instructions Skills Professional Diploma program.

Chain Pet Supply Stores

PetSmart and PETCO, the nation's largest chain pet supply stores, each offers a program to train and employ dog trainers. Many a trainer has gotten their start locally and inexpensively by going through these programs. The companies will put you through a training course, and then have you teach group classes and possibly private lessons at their stores. Visit your local PetSmart or PETCO to watch classes and to get more information on their programs.

Apprenticeship

An excellent way to gain theoretical knowledge and hands-on experience is to apprentice with an established trainer. Trainers who offer group classes will often take on assistants; some will require that you bring your own dog through their classes first. This arrangement is advantageous for both of you—you get first-hand experience with the trainer's techniques, and you both get a feel for whether your personalities and training styles mesh. Don't be discouraged if you find that some trainers are less than friendly when approached. Unfortunately, there are those who take the element of competition very seriously and have less than helpful attitudes toward other trainers. Usually the folks who feel that way are insecure themselves. Keep looking. Experienced, secure trainers who understand that there are enough dogs with behavior problems to go around and that the world needs more good trainers are out there. You will find one who is willing to help you along. A good place to start is at the APDT web site. Click on "Trainer Search" to find contact information for trainers in your area.

Note: If you are planning to teach group classes, observe as many different group class trainers as possible. You might not like everything they do, but you will pick up a lot by just watching them. You might learn new techniques, or gain insights on ways to manage a class or how to better relate to students.

Once you establish a relationship with an experienced trainer, he or she might take you along to private lessons. Depending on the trainer, you could eventually become a paid assistant in group classes, teach the classes for the company yourself, and/or work into doing in-home training for them. The trainer could also bring you along to trainer meetings. Often referred to as Trainer Roundtables, these meetings are for trainers to network, and to share ideas and information. Your mentor might also be able to provide information on events in your area that are not widely advertised.

Gimme Shelter

An excellent way to gain invaluable hands-on experience with dogs is to volunteer at your local shelter or humane society. I strongly urge you to do this, regardless of whether you find an individual trainer or company to work with. There is no education like the one you will get by handling and training the wide variety of dogs that come into a shelter. I spent many hours a week for a few years at my local city shelter, first as a volunteer and then as a volunteer coordinator, training other volunteers. It was an amazing experience that improved my skills on many levels. Shelter work will vastly improve your skills in handling dogs, reading canine body language, and dealing with the public. You might also make contacts that can help your future career.

You might find that the shelter you want to volunteer at already has a trainer present. Great! Observe what the trainer does. You may or may not agree with the training methods, but you can learn something regardless. When you volunteer at a shelter, rather than announcing yourself as a potential trainer, go in with a low-key, helpful, willing-to-do-anything attitude. While some shelters have structured programs to train new volunteers, others have none. Either way, learn and respect the procedures for dealing with the animals and the public.

Note: Shelter work can be difficult emotionally, especially if the facility euthanizes animals that are not adopted. Just remember, the help you are giving the dogs and the experience you are gaining are invaluable.

There are excellent resources available to those who are specifically interested in working with shelter dogs. Trainer Sue Sternberg has written booklets that specifically address temperament testing and training shelter dogs, how to choose a dog from a shelter, and more. (See *Resources*.) There is also an internet discussion list devoted specifically to those who train at shelters. It is a great resource for information and support, and is included in the *Resources* section.

Rescue Me

Closely related to working with shelter dogs is working with rescue groups. Some groups are breed-specific, while others rescue mixed breeds. Research groups in your area. Many groups hold adoption days at local parks or pet supply stores. Stop by and observe, and if you're interested, introduce yourself. Explain that you are just starting your training career and would like to help. Most groups will be happy to take advantage of your services. The fact that you are a new trainer shouldn't be a hindrance. After all, their dogs will be receiving free training, which will only make them more adoptable.

Reading/Viewing

There is a lot you can learn about dog training without ever leaving home. Books, magazines, DVDs and audio or video recordings of seminars are great resources to help kick-start your education. Tawzer Dog Videos (see *Resources*), a fantastic resource for trainers of all levels, sells DVDs of seminars that have been presented on dog training and behavior. A variety of topics is offered, such as how to deal with difficult clients, how to recognize stress signals in dogs, and how to identify breed characteristics. All of these topics are extremely valuable in your becoming a well-rounded, effective trainer.

The *Resources* section also lists books ranging from basic obedience training guides that are geared toward the general public, to textbook types that are more appropriate to the serious student of canine behavior, and many in-between. Read and view as much as you can on a wide variety of dog-related topics. Read non-dog-related books as well, on subjects such as training other types of animals, working with people, family dynamics, and small business management. It will all help your career.

One publication in particular bears mentioning: *The Whole Dog Journal.* This excellent monthly journal consistently offers top-notch articles on training techniques, canine health and nutrition, and rates training books, equipment, dog toys, foods and more. If you find that you lack knowledge in a certain area and can't find the latest research on the topic, for example, treating canine noise phobias, chances are there is a back issue that covers just that topic.

You can even download articles online (see *Resources*). I just renewed my subscription for another two years.

Internet Resources

There is a wealth of information on the internet regarding training, some of which is extremely helpful and some...well, let's say, not so helpful. Use your own judgment and remember that anyone can put up a website, and just because something is in print does not mean it's true. There are, however, some excellent websites that are chock full of useful information. Some store the best posts from mailing lists so anyone can access them. Others list canine behavior problems individually, with ideas on how to solve each one. A few of the sites are listed in *Resources*. You will find many more on your own.

There are many excellent online discussion lists that specifically address training issues. If you are a clicker trainer, check out Clicker Solutions, which focuses exclusively on clicker training. There are many excellent trainers there and loads of great information. Once you find a great email list, you will probably find yourself saving the posts into files on different topics. Of course, the APDT list, accessible to members only, is another source of helpful information.

Other lists cover specific topics such as aggression, or working with shelter dogs. A few are listed in the *Resources* section. A good way to find other lists is to point your browser toward Yahoo Groups (http://groups.yahoo.com). Then do a search for "dog" or "canine" (without the quotations), and whatever aspect you are interested in, for example, "shelter dogs." A selection of lists will come up, along with a description of each. Try them out. You can easily unsubscribe if the list is not a good fit, and you might just get a wealth of helpful information, absolutely free of charge.

Certification

It might surprise you to know that as of the time of this printing, there is no degree or license necessary to become a pet dog trainer. Your Uncle Bob could hang out a shingle tomorrow, announcing Uncle Bobby's Dog Training. Frightening, isn't it? And while some schools offer certifications such as "Master Trainer" after just a few short weeks of training (a dubious practice), up until now, there has not been a central certifying body.

The Certification Council for Pet Dog Trainers (CCPDT) is currently helping to rectify that problem by offering a certification for dog trainers (Certified Pet Dog Trainer, or CPDT) that will hopefully one day be recognized worldwide. Certification requirements include a certain level of experience, passing a written exam, and submitting letters of recommendation from professionals in the field. To renew their annual certification, trainers must acquire "Continuing Education Units" (CEUs) to prove they have attended seminars or other educational events. (For more information, see *Resources*.)

~ * ~ * ~ * ~ * ~ * ~ * ~ * ~ * ~ * ~ * ~ * ~ * ~ * ~ * ~

As I've mentioned, you have chosen a great time to become a dog trainer. There are so many educational opportunities now available, and more that will surely have been created since the printing of this book. The best news is that not only are there more resources than ever available to those wanting to learn to train pet dogs, but that many are based on dog-friendly training methods.

4

Topics to Research

When you first start reading books and watching DVDs about training and behavior modification, the sheer volume of information can seem overwhelming. Don't expect to learn everything overnight; tackle one subject at a time. Research each one not only in books, but by reading articles on the internet and by networking with other trainers. Here are a few topics to start with:

Breed Characteristics

No one expects you to be familiar with every dog breed in existence. Besides, no matter how well you know the common ones, you will inevitably come across a few you've never heard of. I recently saw two Entelbuchers, in separate families living in the same neighborhood, within one month. What are the chances? And I recently met my first Lagotto Romagnolo. (Sounds like a great Italian dessert, doesn't it?) You will find that in your area, certain breeds are popular. My business serves a family-oriented community where many people have Labrador Retrievers and Golden Retrievers. I also serve a more rural area, where I see many Australian Cattle Dogs and other "ranch" type breeds. You might see more hounds, retrievers, bully breeds, or other types of dogs, depending on your geographic location.

Start with the most popular breeds in your area. Research what the dogs were bred to do, which medical problems are common to the breed, and the standard temperament, physical activity level, and whatever else would be applicable to living with that type of dog. If you are well-informed about the dog's breed before each in-home appointment, you will be that much better prepared to answer questions and will impress clients with your knowledge. Understanding the breed groupings and characteristics of each will also help in your training. For example, Beagles are scenthounds, so you'll have a heads-up that getting a super-reliable recall will be important. After all, a Beagle is likely to be distracted by some fascinating scent on the ground while his owner is calling. You'll also know to tell his owner to keep the trash can well covered!

Stages of Development

You will be a much more effective trainer, particularly with pups and younger dogs, if you are familiar with the stages of canine physical and behavioral development. For example, if you know that the period for optimum socialization with other dogs, people and novel stimuli is between four and twelve weeks of age, you can advise clients regarding exposing their pups to those things safely during that period. If you know the teething stage is normally between four and seven months of age, you'll be prepared to offer solutions to a client whose pup is going through that phase. Knowing that adolescence begins at approximately six to seven months of age and lasts until approximately eighteen months to two years can help you to explain to clients how dogs, just like teenagers, gain confidence and challenge boundaries during that time. Many aggression issues, for example, begin during adolescence. There are countless ways your knowledge of canine stages of development will come in handy.

Behavior Issues

There is no way to prepare for every behavior issue that will arise. Even the ones you are familiar with will have variations, and how you approach them may need to be modified, depending on the situation. However, some issues are extremely common and will certainly present themselves.

You should have a basic understanding of how to address:

Housebreaking/Crate training	Stealing
Jumping (on family or visitors)	Door-darting
Barking	Yard escaping
Nipping	Digging
Destruction/Chewing	Counter-surfing

Because you will be working with families, it is also important that you become familiar with common child/dog issues and how to address them. The *Resources* section has some excellent books on the subject.

If you choose to handle more serious behavior issues, your knowledge base should include behavior modification programs for:

Resource guarding (guarding objects/food/locations/people)
Separation anxiety
Fear issues
Aggression toward people
Aggression toward other dogs
Dogs fighting within the home
(Again, handling these types of issues is not mandatory; it's up to you.)

Obedience Training

Begin by learning how to train these basics:

    Attention
    Sit
    Stay
    Down
    Come (a.k.a. "recall")
    Loose Leash-Walking, Heel
    Leave It
    Drop It

Canine Body Language

It is crucial that you become adept at reading canine body language. You will be much more efficient at assisting owners if you can pinpoint (and teach owners to recognize) when dogs are becoming anxious, afraid, frustrated, reactive, potentially aggressive, or displaying a variety of other emotions. I suggest reading some of the wondereful books listed under "Body Language" in the *Resources* section.

A great way to learn about canine body language is to visit your local dog park, film the dogs interacting, then review the footage later. The great advantage of this method is that you can play back sequences over and over, and in slow motion. With practice, your skill at reading canine body language will improve greatly.

Remember too that working with shelter dogs is an excellent way to get a crash course in canine body language!

Pharmacology and Complementary Therapies

As a dog trainer, you are not legally permitted to prescribe medication. It is, however, useful to have a good, working knowledge of drugs and medications that are commonly prescribed for canine behavior issues, especially if you will be working with cases that involve fear and aggression. Sometimes drugs affect canine behavior in ways of which clients are not aware; you should be. Some drugs, for instance, have the potential side effect of intensifying aggressive tendencies. Others that are used to sedate dogs also tend to lower inhibitions, which can translate to abnormal behavior. A familiarity with medications and their uses will allow you to suggest to clients, when appropriate, that they discuss pharmacological intervention with their veterinarian.

Medication should be used as a "foot in the door" to help dogs relax enough that a behavior modification program can begin to work. Over time, when the program has succeeded and the dog's behavior has changed, he can be weaned gradually off the medication.

Become familiar with complementary and alternative therapies as well. Dogs with issues such as fear, aggression, and separation anxiety can be helped by modalities such as Ttouch, acupuncture, acupressure, Bach Flower Essences, homeopathic remedies, nutritional therapy, and other natural aids. See *Resources* for books on these topics.

Building Confidence

A friend of mine is just starting her dog training career. She has read all the right books, watched step-by-step DVDs, and practiced with her own dogs. She works part-time at a shelter, so she has experience working with a variety of breeds and temperaments. She would make a great professional trainer. The trouble is, she lacks the confidence to make the leap to training as an actual job. She feels hesitant about charging money for her skills, which she feels may be underdeveloped—especially when compared to other trainers in her area. You may find yourself in a similar situation. If so, here are some suggestions to bridge the "confidence gap" so you can feel better about beginning to charge for your services.

Phone a Friend

Enlist a friend to help you role-play a training session. She should call you just as a client would, so you can practice your phone skills. Set an appointment. Arrive at your friend's home with the understanding that as long as you are there, you are the trainer and she is the client—no "friend talk" until afterward. Do everything just as you would if she were an actual client. Conduct the session, ask questions, chat, work with the dog, and make recommendations. Schedule another appointment if necessary.

Now, get feedback from your friend. Ask whether the suggestions you made were helpful, if you were clear in your instructions, and for any other constructive feedback. Doing this type of mock session can help you to work out some of the kinks before taking on actual clients, and can give your confidence a great boost.

To the Rescue!

Contact a local rescue group and offer to do a free in-home training session for anyone who adopts a dog from them. Or, offer a free group class to adopters. Since you are not charging for your services, you won't feel so pressured to perform perfectly. Although you will not have to keep sessions to a strict time frame, it will be good practice for getting your pacing down, as your "real" clients will be paying by the hour.

Another type of service you could offer is a free group class for rescue group volunteers. Each volunteer could take a rescue dog through your class. This accomplishes three things: the dogs get training, which makes them more adoptable; the volunteers learn valuable training skills, which they can then use with any dog who comes into the rescue; and you get to develop your skills and gain confidence. A great perk that goes along with offering services to a rescue group is that once you do start charging, you will probably get referrals from them. Be sure to offer adopters a discount!

Rent-A-Trainer

Hire an experienced trainer to come along on an actual in-home visit. Explain to the client in advance that another trainer will be present, and that he/she may have some additional input. The client shouldn't mind. After all, they're getting two trainers for the price of one! The trainer should observe the session quietly, offer helpful advice when appropriate, then give you constructive criticism and feedback in private afterward. Try not to be nervous because of being monitored. The trainer is there to help, and the positive feedback should make you feel more confident.

When All Else Fails

Though it's not likely, imagine that the worst happens: You go to see a paying client, and are faced with a problem you simply cannot resolve. Perhaps the issue is one you were not expecting, or is one you are familiar with, but have never seen presented in quite that way. Relax. If there are other issues that were addressed during the session (as opposed to the problematic one being the sole reason for the call), offer to consult with other trainers and explore other resources, and phone the client back with a solution. If the problematic issue constitutes the entire reason for your visit, as a last resort, you could always offer to refund the fee and apologize for not being able to help with the particular issue. If you know a trainer who is more experienced, refer the client. (See if you can tag along to the session to watch how the trainer handles it.)

The situation might seem awkward, but it is not the end of the world. And people do appreciate it when someone admits he or she doesn't know it all, and refers them to someone who can help. But don't worry—chances are this situation won't come up, and if it does, it won't happen often. In fact, you might be surprised to discover how much you *do* know. As you go along, your skills will improve. You will develop confidence and get better at dealing with novel situations. You *will* be a good trainer!

Take your time, accumulate knowledge and experience, and don't feel cowed by other trainers or compare yourself to them. Someone might have been in the business for over thirty years, but the question is, what has the person learned during that time? Is the trainer still going to seminars, reading books, and keeping an open mind to new information? Or is that person stuck in the same ways of training that were cutting-edge thirty years ago?

Remember: *The best trainers are those who never stop learning!*

Setting Up Your Business

The Red Tape, Nuts N' Bolts "Business Stuff"

If you choose to become an employee of an established training company, you will not have to deal with some of the issues mentioned in this chapter. The responsibility for advertising, record-keeping and other company business will fall to your employer. Your responsibility will be to learn their methods and curriculum, and do a good job of training their customers' dogs.

If you choose to open your own business, even if you will only be a one-person company, there are some important preparations you must make.

DBA (Doing Business As)

Most states require that when you start up a new business, you place a DBA (Doing Business As) notice in the newspaper. This small, inexpensive classified ad announces your business identity to the world. The newspaper will do a search before placing the ad to ensure that no one else in your city is already using the same exact business name—if the name is already in use, that would negate the legality of your using it. The nice thing is, once your ad has been placed, no one in your city can use the name you have chosen. Call your local newspaper for more information, and shop around; rates can vary widely.

Note: Your business name should reflect what you are all about. My business name, "Gentle Guidance," suggests gentle methods. I have had callers say they chose me because of what the name implied. "Take Control K9 Training" reflects a more assertive approach. Avoid generic names. You could use your own name, as in "Jane Doe's School of Doggy Manners." Make your business name stand out so people take notice.

Licensing

Some cities or states require that you obtain a business license, regardless of the type of business you run or the number of employees you have. Others do not require a one-person business without an actual facility to carry a business license. Call your local County Clerk's office to research regulations in your area.

Resale

If you plan to sell training or other supplies to your clients, you will need a resale license. Depending on where you live, you may be required to charge sales tax, and to report that income on an annual tax return. Check with your State Board of Equalization for regulations in your area.

Banking

Set up a separate checking account for your business. A business checking acount will keep your business income and expenditures separate from your personal transactions. That, in turn, will help to keep things better organized for tax purposes. It also looks more professional to have clients make checks out to a business, rather than to you personally. Order an authorization stamp through your bank or rubber stamp store to endorse checks you receive. It should include your business name, bank, and account number. After all, you *will* eventually have too many checks to want to keep signing them manually!

Insurance

Regardless of how small your client base is to begin with, carry liability insurance. You might be an incredible trainer, but this is the real world and, well, dog poop happens. There was a case where a well-known, experienced behaviorist was working with a client's dog in public. The dog severely bit a passerby. The man sued for a million dollars—and won. Although this sort of thing does not happen often, it can happen.

If you plan to teach classes through your local city or county's Parks and Recreation Department, you might find that they require you to carry a million-dollar liability policy. (Don't panic; it won't cost as much as you might think.) They might also ask that you list them as "co-insured." This is standard practice, and protects them in the event that someone sues. Insurance is relatively inexpensive and well worth the cost. Check out exactly what the policy covers. Does it insure you only, or the place where you teach classes as well? Does it cover medical expenses in case a client is injured? Two carriers who will insure dog trainers are listed in the *Resources* section.

Setting Fees

Whether you opt to do group classes, private, in-home training, or a combination, you must consider what to charge. There are no hard and fast pricing guidelines, as rates for dog training vary greatly from region to region. Fees are generally higher in heavily populated, urban areas, and less so in remote regions. The reality is that you can only charge "what the market will bear," meaning what people are willing to pay. Call around to trainers in your area and inquire about their rates. You do not need to announce yourself as a trainer if you don't want to, but could inquire instead as an interested party. If you don't feel comfortable doing that, ask a friend to call around for you. Another option is to seek out websites of trainers in your area, as some will list fees.

Don't purposely try to undercut the competition. It's not ethical, and besides, cheap is not always more attractive to potential customers. Even if you are not intentionally trying to undercut anyone's prices, there is a real tendency when first starting out to charge less, due to a lack of confidence and experience. I am not suggesting that you charge as much as an experienced, well-established trainer, but that you don't sell yourself *too* cheaply. In fact, there is a strange economic phenomenon whereby people think that if something costs more, it's worth more.

If you plan to offer group classes, calculate what you must charge per person, based on the number of dogs allowed in class, to arrive at your desired income. One hour-long group class lesson netted me approximately the same as one hour-long in-home session. Your mileage may vary depending on your class size, venue and geographic location. When calculating, be sure to include the time you spend on class preparation, that is, creating lesson plans, handouts and homework.

When setting fees for in-home training, be sure to take travel time into account. Decide on a basic fee to cover a specific distance. For example, your fifty-dollar-per-hour fee could apply to visiting any home within fifteen miles. Now, take a map and draw a circle with a fifteen mile radius, with your home as the center point. Draw another circle outside of that one, with an additional ten mile radius. Anything that falls between the first and second circles will require, for example, an additional ten dollar travel fee. Keep drawing circles up to the distance you are willing to travel. That way, when callers inquire about areas you are not familiar with, you can easily refer to the map and let them know whether you service the area, and if so, what the charge would be.

I have a trainer friend who simply charges an extra dollar for each extra mile traveled (each way). Through experience, you will come to immediatley know what extra charge, if any, to add on for travel time.

Don't fret too much about fee-setting; nothing is written in stone. If you find people balking at your rates, lower them. If, after gaining more confidence and experience, you choose to raise your rates, that's perfectly appropriate. Take it one step at a time.

The Home Office

Since you are just starting out, let's assume that your office space will be in your home. Designate a room or area of a room as your home office. The most helpful "office supply" to have in this space is a personal computer with a high-quality printer. Following are other essentials.

Home Office Essentials

Financial Software

Purchase a financial software program aimed at small business owners. This will allow you to enter transactions such as income from clients, and business expenses. Record-keeping is essential for tax purposes, and a computerized program makes it easier at tax time by separating items into categories. For example, expenditures could be broken down into Advertising, Training Equipment, Office Supplies, and so forth. There are many software programs that are simple to set up and use, and all will allow you to create charts and graphs so you can track your financial progress.

Get in the habit of saving your receipts for anything and everything that is business-related. If you use your vehicle to drive to clients' homes, part of your car-related expenses are deductible; if you discuss dog training over lunch with your mentor and you pay, the meal is deductible; so are your training supplies. Having a home office may allow you to write off part of your mortgage, phone bills and utilities. Get a list of what is deductible from your tax consultant. Keep a file of your bills and receipts. Remember that with your own business, you are completely responsible for keeping track of all your income and expenses. Once your income begins to grow, you might want to consider paying your taxes quarterly rather than annually so the payment is not overwhelming.

Other Software

A database program is another helpful software tool. Keeping all of your clients' addresses and contact information on file will help to keep things organized. It will allow you to call up a client's information quickly, send invoices or other correspondence, and do a mass printing of address labels for holiday cards or special incentives.

One last program you'll need is a word processing program such as Word, so you can print letters, contracts, attendance sheets, lesson plans, homework for group class, and handouts. Fortunately, pretty much all computers nowadays come with a word processing program.

Answering Machine

In addition to a computer, you will need a phone with a reliable answering machine. Spend the few extra dollars to purchase a quality unit. There is nothing more disconcerting than having someone tell you they've left repeated messages and have been waiting for a return call, when you've never even received the messages. Even worse, you are then left wondering how many other calls you've missed. If you can afford it, an answering service (available through most major telephone companies) is a good option. The obvious advantage is dependability, since it does not rely on the proper functioning of your electrical equipment, and will never cut anyone off mid-message.

Dedicating a second phone line to your business is best, but if necessary, your house line can be used for business as well. (Discuss deduction allowances with your tax advisor.) Your outgoing message should sound friendly and professional, and when you answer the phone, your business name should be spoken in a professional manner.

On The Road

Cell Phone

When you are on the road, a cell phone is essential. It will allow you to call clients when you have been delayed, check your messages and return calls promptly, and of course, to call for help in an emergency. (Have a button preset to call 911.) A cell phone is absolutely worth the expense. Besides, its business use is tax-deductible.

Planner

You will also want to purchase a planner (date book) or electronic organizer to carry with you to training appointments. That way, when you impress the heck out of those clients and they want to schedule another appointment, you can easily schedule it on the spot.

Organizer for Client Information

There are various ways to organize client information. I have a trainer friend who inputs each client's information, including what transpires at each training session, into a hand-held electronic device. She later transfers the information to her home computer. I do not have the faith that these devices will not malfunction, so I do it the old-fashioned way—with a notebook. I carry a three-ring-binder to sessions. I have a sheet for each client that includes contact information, information about the dog, training issues, and space to record what has been done at each session, and any notes. (For a sample client sheet, see *Preparation for In-Home Sessions*.) If a client cancels a session (or if I must cancel), that is noted on the sheet as well. Making these notations will allow you to keep track of how many times someone has cancelled, so you can decide whether to keep working with that client. As a side benefit, the three-ring-binder can serve as a solid barrier, should you ever be greeted at the door by an unexpectedly aggressive dog!

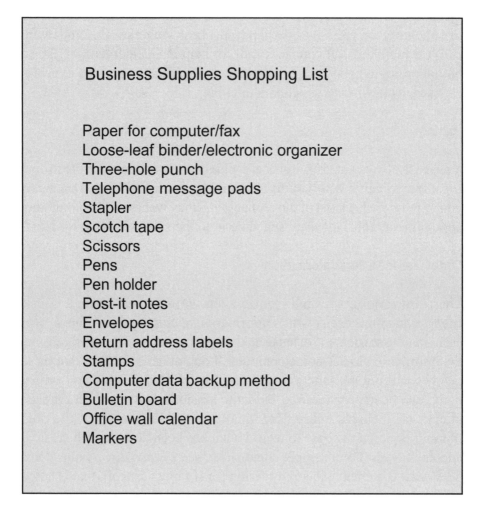

Business Supplies Shopping List

Paper for computer/fax
Loose-leaf binder/electronic organizer
Three-hole punch
Telephone message pads
Stapler
Scotch tape
Scissors
Pens
Pen holder
Post-it notes
Envelopes
Return address labels
Stamps
Computer data backup method
Bulletin board
Office wall calendar
Markers

Preparing Your Printed Matter

We're almost there. Before you start advertising, though, let's prepare some important printed matter.

Contracts

Whether you do in-home training or hold group classes, you should have clients sign a contract. If you teach group classes, it is good practice to send out a contract in advance and ask that it be signed and returned along with a deposit to hold the student's place in class. Private clients should sign a liability waiver before any training takes place, regardless of whether the client does one session or ten.

A contract should spell out clearly and concisely what services the client is entitled to, your refund policy, and should absolve you (at least on paper) of any liability that is not due to your own negligence. I say "at least on paper" because the reality is that a contract might not actually stand up in court. It might, however, lead a client to feel less inclined to sue once it has been signed. For group classes, your refund policy should state that no refund will be given after the first class commences. Of course, you can always choose to give refunds to clients who have extenuating circumstances, but the contract gives you the right *not* to refund monies if you so choose.

A sample copy of a group class liability contract is included in the *Preparation for Group Class* chapter. Feel free to incorporate any part of it into your own contract, or use it as is. You should, however, have a lawyer review *any* contract before use.

Handouts

Client handouts are normally one-sheet summaries regarding a specific topic. For example, I have handouts titled *Basic Principles of Positive Training, Crate Training, An Introduction to Clicker Training, Suggested Reading List, How to Stuff a Kong (Or, Take This Kong and Stuff It!)* (more on Kongs later), *Resource Guarding,* and *Leadership*, among others. Whether in group class or at in-home sessions, clients may be nervous or distracted, and might not retain all the information you want to impart. Handouts leave them with something to refer to, and are also helpful for filling in any details you might have forgotten to mention. You could even create handouts for specific holidays, such as a Christmas handout on the dangers of holiday plants and ornaments, or a Fourth of July handout about dealing with noise phobias.

Homework Assignments

Another type of handout you will need to create if you plan to give group classes is the homework assignment. A good homework sheet reviews what was taught in class, touches on key training points, and offers suggestions on how students should work with their dogs until the next class. For example, if "down" was taught in class using a food lure, the handout might review the luring process, discuss how to fade the food lure, and give specific directions on when, where and how long to practice at each home session. Some trainers distribute handouts at each class, while others combine them into a manual that is given to students at the start of the program.

Form Letters

If you plan to teach group classes, have a form letter prepared to send out to those who sign up, along with the contract. See *Group Class Considerations* for a sample letter.

Coupons

Another type of printout to consider is the coupon. Everybody loves a bargain! Although you should not sell your services too cheaply, offering a one-time, ten-percent discount on a private session or group class won't hurt, and might well draw new clients. Coupons can be offered at any time of year, or be tied in with a specific holiday or event. They can be printed as part of an advertisement, or left wherever your brochures appear around town. You could also present your current clients with an incentive coupon that nets them a discounted future session for each client they refer to you. And of course, discount coupons could go to shelters and rescue groups as well.

The Dog Trainer's Business Kit

Here's where I risk sounding like an infomercial, because I need to tell you about a product I created. Now, anyone who knows me laughs over the fact that I am *not* the self-promotional type. But here's the thing... I spent so many years as a trainer, and perhaps like you, way too much of that time creating contracts and other necessary paperwork. After including some of those documents in my various books for trainers, it occurred to me one day to bundle them together to make life easier for other trainers. And so *The Dog Trainer's Business Kit* was born.

The CD-ROM works on both pc computers and macs (with files in Word, Pages, and .pdf formats), and contains many of the documents you'll need in the day-to-day operation of your business. There are contracts for group lessons, private lessons, and board-and-train, handouts on all the previously mentioned topics, a chart to help clients with homework, intake forms, advance questionnaires, phone message forms, and a whole lot more. You can modify the forms, and add your own business name and logo if you'd like. Check it out at www.phantompub.com. You can even view some of the forms online.

Now that you've got your business set up, policies in place, and printed matter prepared, let's move on to advertising!

9

Advertising Essentials

It's time to let the world know just how much they want your services. Regardless of how small your initial advertising budget, three immediate essentials are brochures, business cards, and a website.

Brochures

Brochures need not use fancy paper, have lots of colors, or be expensive to produce. I designed my own brochure using a typesetting program on my computer. The first year I was in business, I simply printed out as many as were needed at the time. The brochure is a two-sided, tri-fold design with simple black text on 8.5" x 11" pastel-colored paper. It looks professional, clean, and clear, including the black and white photo on the cover. Years later, I still use the same basic design, with slight modifications. I provide my local print shop with the file on disk, and they run off as many copies as I need on plain pastel paper.

You might eventually decide to upgrade to color photos, glossy paper, or heavier card-stock, but there is no need to spend a lot of money at the beginning. As long as the brochure looks attractive and professional, it will get people's attention. Besides, it's what's written inside that will make them want to call you.

If you don't already have one, design a logo to represent your business. Your logo should appear on business cards, brochures, advertisements, your website, and anything else you present to the public. Keep the lines clean and simple. If you are not artistically inclined, hire a graphic designer—it is important that the logo look professional.

Keep the cover of your brochure eye-catching and simple. You could incorporate an attractive photo of yourself with a dog or dogs, or even a cute photo of a dog alone or with a child. The cover should display your business name and contact information, along with a brief announcement of what you do. The front of my brochure, for example, says *"Gentle Guidance"* with my logo just above it, then "Training" in block letters. Underneath that is my catch phrase, "For Dogs and their People." There is a close-up, friendly-looking photo of myself and a Malamute mix, our heads tilted together affectionately. Directly under the photo is "Behavior Specialist," and under that, "Certified Pet Dog Trainer."

When I taught group classes, the front cover also listed (on one line each) "Private, In-Home Training/Behavior Modification/Obedience/Puppy Kindergarten." Now it simply states, "Private, In-Home Training." My name, phone number, and website appear at the bottom, along with a small line that reads "Member, Association Pet Dog Trainers (APDT)." That might seem like a lot of text, but it's spaced out nicely and does not look cluttered. Keep your cover simple. There is plenty of space inside to explain what you do and why you are the best person for the job; but to do that, you need to catch the prospective client's eye first.

Inside the brochure, describe the services you provide. Don't just write a laundry list of your services—make the text really zing! Let people know how you can specifically help them. You might mention some common behavior/training issues so people will see them and think, *Ah, that's just what my dog needs help with!* The first inside panel of my brochure lists common behavior problems, then says at the bottom, "...and most importantly...your dog's specific needs!" The center panel talks about my training philosophy, emphasizing that I train using positive methods, which are effective, and pleasant for both dogs and owners. Be sure to let people know what's special about you and your training, and why you are the best choice over any other trainer they could just as easily hire.

Note: As far as brochure design, I'm partial to the tri-fold. Some trainers prefer to use a third-of-a-page, heavy stock one-sheet. These tall, sturdy cards sometimes have text on the back as well. Either way, be sure your brochure will fit into a standard brochure stand. After all, it will eventually find its way to countertops all over your neighborhood!

The last inside panel of my brochure offers a mini-biography/resume that includes my pertinent experience and qualifications. If you have experience volunteering with a shelter, belong to any dog-related associations, have held dog-related jobs, or have an applicable degree or certification, here's where you should let the world know. Don't be shy, but don't toot your own horn too much, either. I saw a flyer once where the entire three inside panels were covered with the trainer's qualifications and experience. Extensive as they were, there was not a word about how he could help the potential client's dog!

Strike a balance. If you don't have much experience, that's okay. Don't lie about your qualifications, but do play up your good points. Have you always had a way with shy dogs? Great! Someone out there has a shy dog who would love to meet you. Did you ever do family counseling? Very applicable—you have a way not only with dogs, but with people. Even if you have no dog-related experience, list the things about you that are unique, or that will make people remember and want to call you.

Including a warm, friendly touch can help to distinguish your brochure from all the cold, business-like ones out there. Mine has a tag line at the end of the bio section that reads "Nicole is motivated by a true love of canines, and it shows. Her patience, kindness and sense of humor makes training fun and easy for both dog and owner." The idea is for people to understand that not only am I likely to treat their dogs well, but that I will be patient with them, too. They come away feeling that the experience will be pleasant for everyone—and it will!

Don't list prices on your brochure—it doesn't look professional and besides, you might want to adjust them—but do mention any special ongoing offers. For example, "One free in-home session when you register for Group Obedience Class." If you offer specific training programs, mention them. Most trainers in my area sell package deals where customers must purchase a block of six to eight sessions. My brochure offers the alternative, "Go lesson by lesson—get as many private sessions as *you* need." Again, I'm telling the public what sets me apart, and why it is to their advantage to choose me.

As you build a clientele, you may want to include testimonials in your brochure. Testimonials are rave reviews from satisfied customers that will make others want to have the same kind of training experience with you. I do not include testimonials in my brochure because it is already in danger of becoming overcrowded (they're on my web site instead), but if you have them and have the space, include them. I do have one simple oval on the back of the last brochure panel that frames the words, "Referred by more local vets, groomers and pet stores than any other trainer!" Don't make that sort of claim if it's not true, but if it is, don't feel silly or boastful by including it. Statements like that tell the prospective client that local professionals think enough of you to refer their clients to you—a valuable endorsement.

Business Cards

Your business cards should include your business name, logo, slogan if you have one (for example, "Training made fun and easy"), your website, a brief line or two stating your services, and your contact information. That's it. There are an infinite variety of business card designs available, ranging from plain black text on white card stock to multi-colored photos on a holographic background. Keep it simple. Remember, you want your business cards to look professional, but not to cost a fortune.

Rather than getting into the specifics of business card design, I would like to point you toward an excellent book called *How To Market Your Dog Training Business* by Lisa K. Wilson. It was a great help to me when I started out. Wilson gives useful, specific information on designing business cards, brochures, newsletters and mailers, along with samples of each. She also details and gives sample letters of newsletters, news releases and more. The book is available through Dogwise (see *Resources*). Once you have the basic design for your business cards, you can either print them on your home computer on an as-needed basis, or visit your local print shop for larger quantities.

Keep business cards with you at all times. They will come in handy at get-togethers, or anywhere you run into people and start talking about dogs—which, you will find, is just about everywhere! Always leave a few cards with clients so they can keep one and pass the others along.

Website

In today's competitive market, a website is an essential advertising tool, even if you are a one-person business. The first step is to design a simple, attractive site. There are many computer programs available to guide you step-by-step through the process. Or, if you would prefer, hire someone to create a website for you—it is well worth the investment.

Content

Your website should include your business name and logo, the services you offer, and a few words about your training philosophy. It should also give a clear idea of why owners should call *you* instead of the other training companies whose sites they have browsed. Examples of how you might stand out are: "Local resident, recommended by local business owners" or "Force-free methods!" You should also include your qualifications and experience, any media attention you have received (such as copies of newspaper articles) and brief testimonials from satisfied customers. My own site includes these, as well as testimonials from clients, local veterinarians, groomers and other pet-related businesses. List your contact information, including your email address, so people can reach you immediately with inquiries.

If you teach group classes, include your class schedule and location. This will save you the time of providing that information by phone. To simplify things even further, you could include your prices and a downloadable registration form, along with an online payment method. This setup has the advantage of making on-the-spot sales while prospective students are feeling motivated. If you teach private lessons, whether to list your prices is a personal decision. I choose not to list my rates. I would rather establish rapport with a prospective client on the phone, and get a better idea of the dog's issues, before quoting fees. The advantages of including your rates would be that it would screen out people who could not afford them, and would encourage those who could to contact you.

Other things you might choose to include on your website are articles, a blog, information about local pet-related events, and links to other helpful sites. As you will see in the following section, all of those things can be useful in guiding people toward your site.

Domain Name and Hosting Service

A domain name—for example, dogtraining.com—secures your internet identity. (The URL, or address, would be www.dogtraining.com.) However, in order for you to be allowed to purchase the desired domain, it must not already be registered to someone else. Common names tend to get snapped up quickly. There are many sites through which you can do a search to see whether the domain you want is available and, assuming it is, register it so no one else can use it. Paying an annual renewal fee ensures that you remain king or queen of your domain.

You will, of course, also need a "web host" to provide a cyber-rental space for your site to inhabit. There are many that have low monthly rates. Two popular ones are doteasy.com and godaddy.com.

Making Your Presence Known

Once you have created your website, the trick is to help prospective clients find it. Here are a few ways to accomplish that goal:

1. Page Title: Be sure the title of your main page includes words that people will use in search engines. For example, if your business is called "Your Best Friend," it would be better to make the title of the main page "Your Best Friend Dog Training." That way, when people search for "dog training," the title will help the search engines to find your page. Better yet, include your location in the title page as well. In HTML code, the title is inserted between the two title tags. So if you lived in Kansas City, your HTML could read <title> Your Best Friend Dog Training Kansas City </title>.

2. META tags are HTML code that allows you to insert key words and other important information. No one will actually see this information, but it will help the search engines to find your site. The most important tag is "keywords." Think about which words and phrases people might use to search for your services. These might include: dog training; dog behavior; puppy; group classes; training classes; (your city name); and any other specialties you offer, such as "dog aggression." Separate each key word or phrase with a comma, and use different combinations to help people find you. Here is an

example of how this might look in your HTML code: <meta name="Keywords" content= "dog training, puppy classes, dog behavior, dog training Kansas City"> If someone is designing the site for you, you will be asked which key words and phrases to include.

3. Exchange links with other websites. The more places your site is listed, the higher it will rank with the search engines.

4. As mentioned, it is a good idea to include articles on dog-related topics, and information on local events. Let's say your city is having a pet fair. You advertise the fair on your site. When someone goes to a search engine and types in "pet fair," your site will be included in the listing of matching sites. The person visits your site, finds the information she is looking for, and is also made aware of your training services. Now that she knows your business exists, she might hire you in the future, or at least refer others to your site.

5. Search Engines: Each search engine has its own requirements for submitting sites. Go to the popular ones (such as Google and Yahoo) to research individual requirements. There are also sites that will submit your web page to many search engines at once. Some of these services are free, while others are not. It is not necessary to pay to get your website listed. Once you have submitted your site, be patient; it can take a few days to a few months for a search engine to list it.

6. Let's say you write a blog about separation anxiety. Now someone does a search for that topic; the person finds your website, easy as that. Another reason to write (and frequently contribute to) a blog is that it keeps people coming back, and also establishes rapport.

There is a wealth of information available online about how to expand your web presence and get your site ranked higher on the search engines. If you go to Google (www.google.com) and type in "website promotion," "website get hits" or a similar phrase, a listing of helpful sites should appear. Many books are available on the subject as well.

Be sure to include your website on all of your advertising materials, such as brochures, business cards, print ads, and magnetic car signs.

10

All the News that's
Fit to Print

The Print Ad

Print ads run the gamut from small and inexpensive to extravagant and pricey. Some will generate a lot of business, while others will just sit there looking pretty. Research publications in your area and inquire about advertising rates. Consider local newspapers, small neighborhood "pennysaver" type publications, and regional magazines. Be as specific to the area that your business serves as possible. Remember, you will get calls from people in all areas served by that publication. Decide how far you will travel and place your ads accordingly.

There are two main ad types: classified, text-only listings, and display ads. Classified ads are less expensive, so you can afford to run them more often. Find out what your local newspaper offers. Sunday is usually a good day for running classified ads, as many people read that section on weekends. Many newspapers offer packages that include a few other days as well.

Even though a classified ad may be small, it can still garner attention. Create an eye-catching headline, and have it printed in bold type—you don't want your information to be lost in a sea of plain black text. Because your ad will be small, include the most pertinent information only. Depending on the allotted word count, try to include something that makes your business stand out, such as "Small, personalized group classes" or "Free consultations." You might be surprised at how much business a simple classified listing can bring.

A display ad is larger, allows for photos, and will bring in more business. A well-designed display ad should include your business name and phone number, web site, logo, eye-catching text, and, if the space is large enough, a photo. Photos pull readers in and are worth the extra expense. Just be sure not to clutter the ad space with too much text.

Whichever type of ad you choose, check around for special incentives. Some publications offer a monthly or annual rate. Test an advertisement's impact in a particular publication before committing to a long-term agreement, but keep in mind that it usually takes at least three publications of an advertisement for the general public to respond. People typically notice an ad the first time or two, then actually act on it the third time or after. Apparently, repetition is an effective learning tool for people as well as dogs!

Telephone Directory

Another type of print ad that can be very effective is a display ad in your local telephone directory. Rates vary depending on which directory you choose and where you live, but most are fairly expensive. Nowadays there is usually more than one phone directory in any given area—not all pages are Yellow. Other factors that influence cost are size and placement of the ad, whether the print is in color or black and white, background color, photos, and size of the geographic area served. Advertising in a large city's directory will be significantly more expensive than doing so in one that services only a small, rural area. Check the area your phone directory covers, as your responses will come from all over that region. Decide whether the fees are worth the potential clientele. Consider too that even without this type of ad, plenty of potential clients can still find you through your website.

Should you choose to run an ad, keep it simple and eye-catching. I chose to place a Yellow Pages ad with a "knockout" background (the background is white instead of the usual yellow). Knockouts are an excellent and relatively inexpensive way to make your ad stand out. I used two colors (in addition to the standard black) in order to make certain text "pop," and highlighted a few key words by placing a starburst around them. The ad was not large enough to include a photo, but I did use my logo, and, with the help of the directory's art department, designed a simple, eye-catching piece that has been very effective. I did go back and forth with the art department quite a few times until I was satisfied with the results. Don't feel guilty or pushy if you end up doing the same. That's what they're paid for, and besides, you'll be living with the results for a whole year. Many directories offer discounts to first-time advertisers, so be sure to shop around.

Press Release

Another way to use the power of the printed word is to issue a press release. It won't cost you a thing, and is an excellent way to get the word out about your business. Although your goal is to advertise, a press release should not read like an advertisement; it's more like an "advertorial," a combination advertisement/editorial. For example, you could call your article "New Dog Training Business Opens In (Your Town)." Highlight the services offered, and explain how this fabulous business will benefit the community. On the following page you will find a copy of the press release I used when first announcing my business. Because I also offered puppy classes at the time, I titled another one "Pups Get Off on the Right Paw at Puppy Kindergarten." It discussed how early socialization with other dogs and people benefits puppies. Naturally, my contact information appeared at the end of the article.

Slant your press releases in such a way that they are likely to grab the attention of the average pet owner. Once people read about how helpful socialization and training are, and about other fascinating topics you choose to include, they will want to call for more information. Contact your local paper to find out to whose attention the press release should be sent. (See Lisa Wilson's book for other sample press releases.) Releases can be mailed, faxed, or emailed, although there is an increasing trend toward the use of email for this purpose.

ATT: PAT AIDEM
FAX: (555) 254-5970

FOR IMMEDIATE RELEASE
Contact: Nicole Wilde (800-555-1234/
info@gentleguidance4dogs.com)

Dogs Love to Learn with Gentle Guidance

Gentle Guidance, a Santa Clarita-based dog training company, trains dogs and their owners. Whether in private, in-home sessions or group classes, owners learn to communicate better with their dogs, and dogs learn to listen. Both learn that training can be fun!

"Fortunately, dog training has come a long way since the old days of choke chains and harsh corrections," said owner and Training Director Nicole Wilde. "With gentle, positive methods, dogs not only behave better, but actually enjoy the training process. Reward-based methods also strengthen the dog-owner bond. We love our dogs—so why would we train any other way?"

Wilde has worked with all types of canines (including wolves and wolf hybrids) in both training and rescue for many years. Her work as Volunteer Coordinator with the Los Angeles city shelters, where she socialized and trained dogs and taught volunteers about canine behavior, resulted in hundreds of dogs finding loving homes.

"It's a sad fact that many of the reasons dogs are given up boil down to a lack of training," Wilde said. "So many people don't bother to train their dogs until problems have already developed. Even then, it's never too late. We give our dogs treats, toys and affection. But for a long, happy life together, training is really the best gift of all."

For additional information on Gentle Guidance's dog training services, call 800-555-1234 or visit www.gentleguidance4dogs.com.

11

Other Ways to Advertise

Flyers

A flyer contains the same basic information as a brochure, in simplified form. Your flyer should state briefly what you do, and display your logo, perhaps a photo, and tear-off sheets (small bits of paper than can be torn from the bottom so the whole flyer doesn't get removed). Tear-offs should always include your business name and website, rather than a phone number alone. Otherwise, when Joe Potential Client empties his pockets a week later, he's likely to say "What's this?" and throw it away. (Not to mention the strife it might cause between he and Mrs. Joe!) You can easily produce a mini-flyer by printing four copies of the same design on an 8.5 x 11 page, then slicing it into quarters. Placing four flyers on a page will save you money in reproduction costs, and allow you to post in areas where larger flyers will not easily fit.

Be creative in your placement. Though bulletin boards at pet supply stores, groomers and vets are obvious choices, they are likely to be covered in flyers from other trainers. Post at those businesses, but be creative, too; target places like laundromats, where people have nothing to do but stand around and read the bulletin boards. Apartment complexes that allow pets are another good choice, and usually have communal posting areas. What about supermarkets? Beauty salons? I even know of one trainer who convinced her local pizza shop to deliver her a copy of her flyer with every pizza. The sky's the limit and the advertising is free, so go for it!

Advertising in Motion

One of the best things I ever did for my business was to buy magnetic car signs. The signs announce my services on the way to and from appointments and whenever my vehicle is parked on the street, and they work overtime when I'm driving around town on my days off. I always try to park where people can see the signs, even when I'm going to a movie or a restaurant. I have had people strike up training-related conversations at the gas pump; call out the window from an adjacent car at a red light that they will call me about their dog; and copy down the number as they walk by. I've also had a few people call and say, "I saw your car parked at my neighbor's house. We need help, too!"

As with any advertisement, keep the design clear and simple. A local printer advised me not to clutter the signs with too much text. He was right. We used only the business name, logo, slogan, phone number and website. He suggested two colors on a white background. The result? An attractive, easy-to-read sign for each door. I have since noticed signs on vehicles that display so much information that the tiny print makes it difficult to read—a big mistake if your goal is to attract clients on the go.

My car signs have long ago paid for themselves in training appointments. I personally think they are well worth it and besides, you can always remove them temporarily if the situation warrants it.

Promotional Items

A great way to advertise your business is to give away promotional items imprinted with your business name, logo (if space allows) and contact information. Depending on the size and value of the item (and your budget), promos can be given to each client you see, used as prizes or graduation gifts in group class, as thank-yous for referrals, or as holiday gifts. As a trainer who sometimes uses clickers, I give clickers to many of my clients. You can bet my information is imprinted on them! Ordering in bulk allowed me to get a great price, and it's good to know that clients will literally have my number "handy" to pass along to others.

Another promotional item I hand out regularly is refrigerator magnets. I ordered mine from an online company that offers designs that are specific to pet-related businesses. The one I chose has a Cocker Spaniel in a boot; it frequently elicits exclamations of, "How adorable!" Give magnets to private clients and graduating group class students. When I return to clients' homes, I often notice my magnet stuck on the refrigerator. Fridge magnets are a handy way for clients to keep track of you for future training and referrals.

Other promotional items include t-shirts (a bit more expensive to produce), caps, pens, and coffee mugs. In the *Resources* section, I have listed a few sources for imprinted clickers and refrigerator magnets. There are many companies that specialize in promotional items for businesses. Search for them online and review their catalogs; you might get some unique ideas for promoting your business.

Other Options

Research other ways to get your name out to potential clients. Look into money-mailer type services, where batches of coupons are mailed directly to homeowners. The services may be pricey, but they can target specific neighborhoods in which you want to work. Some are mailed to residents only, while others are sent to businesses as well. Inquire about specifics. If you choose this option, be sure to offer a discount, such as "20% Off Group Classes with this Coupon!"

Most rescue groups hand out an information packet with each adoption. Your brochure should be in every packet! Will your local shelter allow you to place a stand with brochures at the counter? What about offering free talks at the shelter? Subjects could include Choosing a Dog, or Common Behavior Issues. Naturally, you'll have business cards and brochures on hand for prospective clients. Many rescue groups also have sections on their web site that list local trainers. Ask to be added to their listings.

There is no better advertisement than a well-trained dog. Just hanging out at the park with your dog, who is doing tricks and behaving beautifully, is sure to trigger training-related inquiries. Or, what about giving a free demonstration at the park or in front of a shop? You could talk about the importance of having a well-trained dog, or if you're a clicker trainer, dazzle 'em with a live demo of what's possible with clicker training. You're sure to pick up a few clients from impressed passersby.

Research businesses, shelters and animal-related events in your area, then brainstorm about how you can let them know about your services.

Track Your Success

Whenever you take a phone call from a potential client, ask how the person was referred. Keep track of how many calls you get from each advertising source. That will help you to decide whether to keep running print ads, renew your phone directory ad, know that your car signs have been noticed, or whether vets or pet stores are referring to you. Based on the feedback you get, adjust your advertising campaign so it will continue to be effective.

Pleased to Meet You

Now that you've got your business set up, advertising in place, and handouts prepared, it's time to introduce yourself to the community.

Veterinarians

Referrals from veterinarians can account for a large percentage of your business. A recommendation from a vet is an especially valuable endorsement, as dog owners really trust their vets. Call vet's offices in your area and ask whether there is a trainer they refer to. (Or, you could check things out by stopping by in person to see whether there are brochures on display.) When I called around, if a receptionist answered that they did not have a trainer to refer clients to, I exclaimed, "That's great, because I happen to be a dog trainer and I would love to meet you!" More often than not, I was able to make an appointment to visit and introduce myself.

When dealing with vet clinics, be friendly and pleasant with the front office staff as well as the vet. After all, the staff are the ones who will be referring people to you (or not!) and answering questions when people see your brochure. It is good practice to drop by periodically with boxes of cookies or other goodies just to thank the staff for the referrals. As always, there's nothing wrong with a little positive reinforcement!

If, when you call around, you are told the clinic already refers to a trainer, ask whether it is an exclusive arrangement. If not, they might still be open to meeting with you. At the very least, they might allow you to place your brochures in the waiting room along with the others.

Groomers and Others

Groomers are often happy to have a trainer to refer to. Their customers ask for referrals periodically, but many groomers are not aware of trainers in the area. You can easily change that. If you prefer not to cold call, bring your own dogs in for grooming, then strike up a training-related conversation. The same applies to pet supply stores. Chat with the clerk or owner the next time you go in to purchase supplies, and find out whether a trainer is affiliated with the store. If you plan to offer group classes, the store could be a potential venue.

Doggy daycare centers are another great source of referrals. Unless there is already a trainer on site, they should be happy to have a good one in the community to refer to. The same goes for boarding kennels. Whether you're approaching a vet, groomer or any other business, it never hurts to mention that your clientele are local, and that you would be happy to refer to them in turn. (Don't do this unless you really mean it. People mention who they were referred by, and it will become obvious if you're just paying lip service.) You could end up with an arrangement that is mutually beneficial.

Stock Up

When a business agrees to let you display your brochures and/or business cards, supply holders to keep them in. Inexpensive lucite stands do nicely for brochures, and there are a variety of inexpensive cardholders; both can be purchased at any office supply store. Place a sticker on the back of each with your business name and phone number so the business can call you if the supply runs out. This practice also stops others from appropriating your empty holders.

Visit periodically, have brief, pleasant chats with those who are referring to you, and be sure to keep those brochures/cards stocked. You might even want to make a schedule that lists each place your cards and brochures are displayed, and the last date you stocked them. This is especially helpful for keeping track if your materials are displayed at many different places around town.

13

When Business Calls

Telephone Tips

With advertising in place, you'll soon be receiving phone calls inquiring about your services. Here are some tips on how to handle calls effectively:

1. The outgoing message on your answering machine should be clear, friendly and professional. Be sure your live greeting sounds the same. Once you have set business hours, let the machine pick up before and after. Even if you are a one-person company, do not give the impression that you are available at all hours—it's unprofessional. You wouldn't call a doctor at home at any time of the night, and you shouldn't be expected to take off-hour calls either, unless it's an emergency. You could state your availability on the answering message, for example, "Your call is important to us. Please leave a message and your call will be returned during business hours, 9:00 a.m. to 7:00 p.m., Monday through Saturday. We look forward to speaking with you." That way, if someone calls on a Saturday night, a return call would not be expected until Monday morning. Or, if you absolutely do not want to limit your hours at the beginning, leave an approximate time frame within which callers can expect a call back, for example, "Your call will be returned within twenty-four hours."

2. Return calls promptly. My personal goal is to return calls within three to four hours. If you are out all day, check your machine periodically for messages. I have had numerous clients who had called other trainers and never even received a return phone call. That's not only rude, it's bad business. Return all calls, even if the issues are not ones you would normally handle. You might be able to refer the caller to someone else who can help, which might result in the caller referring others to *you* in the future, since you were so helpful.

3. Keep a phone log or notebook near the phone. Each time you receive a call, log the date, client's name and phone number, dog's name, breed and age, how the caller was referred, and what the call is regarding. Once you have discussed rates and availability, some callers will want to confer with their spouses before setting an appointment. Make a note of that, or any other outcome. For example, "Appointment set for (date)" or, "Going on vacation, will call me next week." If you haven't logged the details, unless you have a photographic memory, you'll be faced with appearing clueless when the person calls back. Notes are a great aid. If you get a caller saying, "My name is Denise, I called two weeks ago..." by the time she's finished speaking, having looked through your notes, you could say, "Ah yes, Denise with the Bichon who has housebreaking issues." It makes callers feel good that you "remember" who they are.

Recording call details will also help you to monitor the productivity of your print ads and other referral sources, and to keep track of how many calls resulted in appointments. If most of your calls result in appointments, great! If most don't, take a second look at whether your rates, phone skills or other factors might be playing a part.

4. Potential clients will often begin a phone conversation by saying something like, "Hi, how much would it be to train my dog?" Never quote your rates right away—establish a personal connection first. I usually reply with, "I'd be happy to give you that information. Let me ask a few questions so I can give you an accurate quote. First, do you live in the area?" Assuming so (if not, I will refer to another trainer and save us both a lot of time), I ask what breed of dog the person has, and the dog's age. I then ask, "And how can I help you? Are you looking for basic obedience and manners training, or does your dog have a behavior issue?" Only after we've talked for a few minutes and I have established that I am professional, friendly, knowledgeable, and experienced (and I have found out about the dog's issues), will I quote my rates. After all, if the person is calling around and you answer with your rates right away, there is no reason to choose you over other trainers unless your rates are cheaper. Convince callers in those first few minutes that *you* are the one they want, regardless of rates. They might well decide to book you on the spot, rather than continuing their search. After all, they've already found the best trainer for the job!

5. While it's advantageous to draw potential clients into conversation, once you get certain people talking about their dogs, it can be difficult to get them to stop. Although you need to know what the dog's behavior problem is, you don't want to spend half an hour on the phone hearing about how, "Scout came from a lovely couple who had an accidental litter, and was doing great until Aunt Fanny visited, then it all started falling apart, and Brandon, who's ten by the way, says..." You must learn the fine art of interrupting without sounding like you are trying to cut a client short. I have used phrases like, "You know, that's fascinating and I'd love to hear more about it when I see you. Let's go ahead and book an appointment."

6. Some people love to shop around. You will learn to recognize a phone call from the "Comparison Shopper." She typically wants lots of information, but won't commit to making an appointment. She may even tell you she's already spoken to such-and-such company and their prices are lower, or they gave her some suggestions and would like your take on what they said. While there's nothing wrong with someone wanting to find the best person for the job, don't let the Comparison Shopper monopolize your time. Spend a reasonable amount of time answering her queries, then offer to set up an appointment. If she declines, ask her to call back when she's ready to do so.

7. Closely related to the Comparison Shopper is the "Information Mooch." This guy is not really looking to make an appointment with you or anyone else, ever. He figures that as a professional trainer, you should be willing to answer his questions over the phone, free of charge, for as long as he likes. There is nothing wrong with giving someone a quick, simple solution to a problem that doesn't require an in-home appointment; just don't let the Information Mooch suck you into a long, involved conversation about his dog's issues without making an appointment.

8. When you quote your rates, be specific about the fees and what they cover. For example, let's say your rate for in-home training is fifty dollars an hour, and the first appointment normally lasts an hour and a half. Don't just say, "My rates are fifty dollars an hour" and assume that clients will do the math. Once you've completed a ninety-minute session, the person might be surprised to hear that the total is seventy-five dollars, rather than fifty. Many people hear that hourly rate and tune out the rest, which

could lead them to believe the entire session will cost them fifty dollars, regardless of the length of the session. It is far better to lay it out clearly at the start. For example, "My rate is fifty dollars per hour. The first session usually lasts an hour and a half, so that would be seventy-five dollars for the first session. Lessons after that last one hour only, so they would be fifty dollars each."

If you sell packages of sessions, let callers know up front how many sessions they would be expected to purchase, and how much they could potentially save by doing so. If you sell individual sessions, make it clear there is no further obligation after the first session.

A word about negotiating your rates—*don't*. If a caller is interested but says the rate I've quoted for ninety minutes is a bit steep, I might say, "I understand that money can be an issue. What I can do is keep the first session to an hour so it would only cost you ___. Would that work?" What I will *not* do is drop or negotiate my rates. It is one thing to decide in advance to give a discounted rate to someone who has adopted from a rescue or shelter, or has extenuating circumstances. Letting someone talk you down from your original quote, however, is not only unprofessional, but will earn you a client who is most likely not going to value your advice as much, will forever be trying to get more out of you at less cost, and will haggle about the actual training as well.

It is a strange phenomenon in American culture that many people feel the things we pay for are valuable, while those given away free are not. Be careful about where you place your charity. Working with someone as a favor because she's strapped for cash right now and you feel badly for the dog could lead to you spending lots of time and effort, and the person not really valuing your advice. After all, it was free. It's great to offer free classes at shelters or to work with rescue dogs gratis, but beware of offering free training where it's not likely to be taken seriously or appreciated.

9. Do not make guarantees. While it is tempting to tell a client that you know the dog's problem is absolutely solvable, no matter how strongly you feel it is, don't guarantee it. Dogs are living beings and there is no way anyone can guarantee their behavior one hundred percent—and, you

cannot guarantee that the owner will follow your advice. When asked if you can guarantee that you can fix a behavior problem, reply with something along the lines of, "I've dealt with this same issue many times and have not yet found a case where I couldn't put it right." That's different than saying, "I absolutely guarantee I will fix your dog's behavior problem." The former inspires confidence. The latter could inspire a lawsuit.

10. Try not to feel pressured into taking on any case with which you are not comfortable, whether it's because the behavior issue is out of your area of expertise, someone is not willing to pay your full fee, or for any other reason. People will call you with all sorts of stories, wanting you to do things that are totally outside the scope of your business. Just the other day, a woman phoned me regarding her Bichon's barking problem. She lived in an apartment, was gone all day, and the poor dog emitted a high-pitched bark for hours on end. The neighbors were complaining. I told her I would be happy to set up an appointment. She informed me that she'd already spent a lot of money on another trainer who was not able to solve the problem, and if she didn't fix the problem within the next three days, the dog was to be debarked. Now, at this point I would counsel you that you are running a business, and no matter how bad the situation, you should not allow yourself to be pressured into giving free advice. I will admit, however, that I ended up on the phone with that woman for half an hour doing just that, as the thought of that little dog being debarked horrified me. What I'm saying is, while it's good to have compassion and to do what you can, try not to feel pressured into doing things you don't want to or really shouldn't do on a regular basis. As always, if the issue involves aggression or any other behavior that you are not comfortable dealing with, refer the case to another trainer.

11. After establishing that the caller is a good prospective client, that is, the dog's problem can be addressed with the services that you offer, and your rates and availability are acceptable, it's time to "ask for the sale." While I am in no way a fan of the hard sell (in fact, it really turns me off), you must be a bit of a salesperson. Instead of asking, "Would you like to make an appointment?" (which leaves them the option of choosing not to) say something like, "Are you normally available during the weekdays?" You're not being pushy, you're being efficient. If someone really sounds unsure, I don't push it. Some might disagree with this, believing you

shouldn't take anything but "yes" for an answer, but I have found that pushing someone to make an appointment when there's no real commitment only leads to a cancellation as the day approaches. Don't worry if the "selling" aspect seems awkward at first; as you go along, you'll develop your own style.

12. Try to schedule appointments when the whole family can attend. It is more productive as far as clarity and compliance for spouses and children to hear instructions directly from you, the professional, than second-hand from each other. Plus, you can gain valuable information by observing each family member's interactions with the dog. Having children present can be especially useful, since kids often blurt out useful information that parents wouldn't necessarily offer!

13. If you get an uneasy feeling about someone on the phone for any reason, ask a *lot* of questions. Every now and then, I get "weird vibes" on the phone from a male caller. If that happens, I ask a *lot* more questions than I normally would, such as where the dog came from, how long the dog has been in the home, why the breed was chosen, and more. My initial hesitancy is usually dispelled. If it's not, I find some excuse to turn down the appointment. (If you are on the spot and can't think of an excuse, say someone is at your door, and that you'll call back. That will buy you some time.) Listen to your gut feelings and don't ever take an appointment you feel wary about just because you need the business. It's not worth it. (For more on staying safe at appointments, as well as how to handle difficult callers, see *It's Not the Dogs, It's the People!* in *Resources*.)

Trainer Etiquette

Just as a friendly, knowledgeable phone manner will impress clients, a professional in-person presentation will continue the good impression.

Punctuality

Wear a watch, and always arrive at your in-home appointments and group classes on time. While being delayed by traffic or other unavoidable circumstances is understandable, if you are going to be more than five minutes late, call to let your clients know. If you are teaching a group class, apologize when you arrive. If you have a day with more than one consecutive in-home appointment scheduled, try to end each session promptly so you can stay on schedule. One session that runs twenty minutes over can delay your appointments for the rest of the day.

Appearance

In the dog training business, no one expects you to show up in a three-piece suit. However, appearance and personal hygiene are the first things people notice. Let's take two trainers, Mr. A and Ms. B. Mr. A is roughly forty pounds overweight. That's no crime, except that the way his dirty T-shirt rides up over his belly, you'd think he was proud of the fact. His jeans have tears at the knees, and his hair is perfect...that is, for an off-Broadway production of *Grease*. As Mr. A leans forward to shake the client's hand, it becomes obvious that he prefers his cheeseburgers loaded with onions. What an impression, and the training hasn't even begun! Ms. B, on the other hand, arrives wearing a clean polo shirt emblazoned with her company name and logo, and crisp jeans. Her hair is washed and tied back neatly. Her breath is fresh. She appears friendly, alert and ready to work. Which trainer would *you* want at your home? Don't be lazy. First impressions count. (Personally, I'm so paranoid about bad breath that I always pop a breath mint before walking into a client's home!)

Note: The majority of in-home clients will offer to shake your hand at the door. While in human language this clearly conveys, "Pleased to meet you," to a dog who is protective of his owner, it might mean something else entirely. In fact, the dog might take your reaching toward his owner as a serious threat, and you could be bitten. I'm not suggesting that you never shake anyone's hand, but that you be well aware of the dog's body language before you do. There is nothing wrong with saying, "Please don't think I'm being rude, but I would just as soon not shake your hand, as I can see that it might make your dog uncomfortable." Rather than being offended, the person will probably be impressed that you are so observant of the dog's body language.

Keeping Track of Time

If you find the big hand inching past the hour mark on a scheduled hour-long in-home appointment, call the client's attention to it. No one wants to be surprised by extra charges. When a session is in danger of running into overtime, say something like, "I'd love to show you that exercise we discussed, but we will end up going past the hour. If we go another extra half hour, the fee will be ___ total. Is that okay? If not, we can pick up where we left off at the next session." Always give the client the choice. If you have trouble keeping track of time, set a watch alarm for ten minutes before the scheduled end of the session.

Be Polite

It is good practice to be polite to clients, whether in a group or one-on-one. But trust me, there will be clients who even Martha Stewart would be tempted to strangle (though she'd probably use a freshly pressed tie to do it!). Though the majority of clients you will deal with will be pleasant, inevitably there will be some who will be argumentative, rude, ignorant, annoying, or any combination of the above. Remain polite. Do not allow yourself to be drawn into an argument. After all, you're the professional.

Read up on dealing with difficult people. In any customer service industry the same client types exist, and some wonderful books have been written on the subject. (Also, see *Resources* for a few that are specifically geared toward dog trainers.) Regardless of how hot-headed a client gets, keep your cool. Many argumentative clients, when faced with your cool composure, will calm down themselves. Just as you would not respond to an aggressive dog by countering with force, don't do so with an angry client and risk escalating the confrontation. Use positive reinforcement techniques! Sometimes just reiterating what the person has said can be helpful: "I can understand how frustrating it must be to come home and find urine on the carpet. So, instead of continuing to rub your dog's nose in it, why don't we talk about crate training and management. That way things will become much less stressful right away." Of course, this should be said in a calm, soothing voice. Calm and soothing is helpful when responding to stressed and unbalanced, plus you have let the client know that his concerns have been heard. Call a friend after the appointment or group class and vent if you need to!

If a client's rudeness involves something like responding to one phone call after another during an in-home appointment, politely suggest letting the machine pick up the calls. After all, you want the client to get the most out of the session (and for you not to want to tear out your hair). If the problem involves kids who are throwing tantrums or constantly interrupting, suggest that the parent give them something else to do, like coloring or playing a video game in another room. After all, you'd give a puppy who was chewing on the carpet something else to do—dog-training and kid-training aren't all that different.

Another aspect of being polite is remaining quiet and listening while someone is speaking. Many of us are already thinking of the next question we want to ask as the client is answering the current one. As time is always an issue, it's hard not to interrupt. You may find this especially challenging if, like me, you are a high-energy, stay-on-track sort of person. If necessary, jot your next question down so you can concentrate on what the client is saying and not feel that you have to interrupt; you might just catch a piece of information that is crucial to solving the dog's problems.

While waiting for another person to finish speaking is polite, some clients will launch into lengthy stories about their dogs or about completely unrelated topics. You will have to reel them in. When you sense an opening, gently guide the conversation back to the subject at hand. You could always say something like, "You know, that's really interesting and I'd love to hear all about it, but we only have another fifteen minutes and I want to make sure we get to all the topics we wanted to cover today." It is especially important not to allow people to chat on and on during group classes, as that would monopolize your time and could throw the entire class off schedule.

Be Honest

If clients ask questions you don't know the answer to, it's perfectly fine to say so. While you are expected to know certain things, if you get stumped, just respond with something like, "That's a good question, and I'd like to give you a great answer, so I'm going to consult with one of my colleagues and get back to you." Of course, if a question is totally out of your area of expertise, say so, and if possible, refer them to a source that is likely to have the answer. If the question involves a medical issue, explain that you are not qualified to give veterinary advice, and refer them to their veterinarian. If it is something simple like, "Do you know any good remedies for dry skin?" and you do, go ahead and answer. But answering a question like, "Do you think I should put my dog on Rimadyl for hip dysplasia?" can get you in trouble. You are not qualified to give veterinary advice, and could end up being sued if something goes wrong. Even when recommending natural remedies, suggest that clients clear it with their veterinarians first.

If You've Got Nothing Nice To Say...

Turns out your mother was right. If you don't have anything nice to say, don't say anything at all. It's awfully tempting, when a client mentions another trainer who you know to be an awful trainer, abusive to dogs, offensive to people, or some other unpleasant characteristic, to jump right in and skewer that person along with them. Or to vent when someone asks how you like a popular trainer on television whose methods you just don't argree with. Don't do it! Speaking poorly of others only makes *you* look bad, and is completely unprofessional. Besides, what does it accomplish?

I often answer negative comments about other trainers with a nonchalant, "Everyone's got their own methods. I'm glad to have the opportunity to show you what's worked for me time after time." If a point-blank question is posed to you about another trainer, for example, "What do you think about So-and-So?" as a last resort you could always say, "I prefer not to discuss other trainers" and leave it at that.

If someone asks about a veterinarian who you do not think highly of, instead of saying, "Oh, I've heard terrible things about him!" respond with, "I don't have any personal experience with him, but here's the name of someone I do know and think is wonderful." There is a trainer in my area who used to get lots of referrals from a local veterinarian. This trainer spoke poorly of the vet to a lot of his clients. (Not terribly bright, considering the clients were referred by the vet in the first place!) Word got back to the vet. He is currently suing the trainer for slander. So you see, it really does pay to be pleasant and to keep your tongue in check. Besides, the people who spend the most time putting others down are usually insecure themselves. Rise above it, and concentrate on improving your own skills and reputation.

15

Your Toolbox

In the "Member Profile" section of the APDT newsletter, one of the original questions was, "What's in your toolbox?" No, it doesn't refer to screwdrivers and wrenches, but the Training Toolbox—collars, leashes, clickers, toys, treats, and anything else the trainer keeps on hand. Your toolbox should include items that are proactive, in that they keep dogs busy so they do not get into trouble in the first place. It should contain management tools, educational materials, and helpful products. You will find your toolbox expanding over time, along with your knowledge and experience.

Many items in my toolbox are things I use with my own dogs; they have helped a lot of my clients' dogs as well. I have included a few of them in this section. If you can't find the recommended items at your local pet supply store, try the *Resources* section, or one of the many suppliers who advertise in catalogs or online. So without further ado, to borrow a line from Julie Andrews, "These are a few of my favorite things!"

Interactive Food Toys

For dogs, mental stimulation is just as important as physical exercise. It gives them something to focus on, and tires them out. Teach clients how to provide their dogs with mental stimulation through the use of interactive food/treat dispensers. These dispensers are great for keeping dogs busy during times like the morning get-the-kids-ready-for-school and get-ready-for-work family "rush hours," when there are visitors, and in the evenings when everyone just wants to relax. Some dispensers can be used to feed meals, even if the meals consist of canned food in addition to or instead of dry kibble, while others are best used with dry kibble alone, or to dispense dry treats between meals.

The Kong®

I often joke that I should be working for the Kong® Company. I so love their products that I recommend them to just about every client. My favorite, the Classic Kong®, is shaped like a snowman. It comes in a variety of sizes, and two colors: standard red, and black for tougher chewers. The wonderful thing about the product, besides that it bounces unpredictably, is that it has a small hole at the top and a large one on the bottom, both of which can be stuffed with treats. Dogs will spend a considerable amount of time and effort attempting to get the stuffing out—you can even freeze or microwave food treats in it. My own dogs, who weigh between 80 and 120 pounds, spend upwards of thirty minutes excavating when I pack the stuffing tightly, and trust me, it's not easy to find something that will keep my steel-jawed fur-kids busy that long!

Clients who feed a mixture of wet and dry food can feed their dogs' meals in the Kong®. It's simple to mix wet and dry together, then spoon the mixture into the ball. Or, alternating layers or wet and dry can be used. My mealtime Kong-stuffing technique is on a handout I give to clients, along with other recipes and ideas. There are some great recipes for Kong-stuffing on the company's web site (see *Resources*). The tips are also available by request in the form of a pamphlet called *Recipe for the Perfect Dog*, which you can distribute to your in-home clients and group class students.

Kongs® can be especially useful for dogs who are left alone for long periods, or suffer from separation issues. A yummy Kong® presented just as an owner leaves the house can help to alleviate a dog's home-alone anxiety. It can also help to calm dogs who must be crated. I have one client who calls this magical product a "puppy pacifier," and she's right! There are plenty of things a puppy won't get into while intent on excavating that buried treasure, and as all puppy parents know, not having to watch a puppy every moment is a beautiful thing.

At in-home training sessions, I often stuff the tiny hole at the top with a chewy treat, so clients can see first-hand how intensely their dog tries to get it out, and how busy it keeps the dog. (This also gives me a chance to speak with the client uninterrupted.) It's as though the dog goes into a Zen-like state—and I have only stuffed the small hole! Most clients run out to buy the product after the session, and their dogs couldn't be happier. It's a good idea to have a few on hand for group classes as well. It's amazing how far one rubber ball stuffed with peanut butter can go to calm a dog who is barking or stressed out, thereby keeping the peace in class.

The same company that makes these fabulous interactive food/treat dispensers now offers a creative way to dispense them. The Kong Time™ dispenses Kongs® at random times throughout the day, up to eight hours. You simply pre-stuff the four balls that come with the unit, using your dog's meal divided into four portions. This product may well be the perfect solution for dogs who engage in boredom-induced destruction while owners are gone.

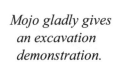

Mojo gladly gives an excavation demonstration.

Buster Cube®

Here we have another great keep-em-busy tool. The Buster Cube® is a hard plastic "dice" with a hole on one side and four chambers inside. Just pour kibble or small, dry treats into the hole, then shake to distribute the goodies throughout the chambers. The insertion hole can be turned to increase or decrease the difficulty level. The dog then paws and rolls the cube around to make the treats fall out. For clients who feed dry kibble, the entire meal can be fed in the cube. Why feed dogs from dishes when they can spend all that time and energy working for it? My own dogs love it when they get their meals this way, and your clients will love the fact that their dogs, especially the super-active breeds, are getting all that energy out in a productive way.

This device is the perfect choice for extremely intelligent dogs who are good at problem-solving. However, the cube is made of a very hard plastic and might not be the best choice if someone has an extremely strong, rambunctious dog and/or antique or fragile furniture. A friend's Pit Bull likes nothing better than to whack the cube into the wall repeatedly, and Mojo has actually disemboweled one or two. Still, for any but the most destructive dogs, the Buster Cube® is a good choice.

Buster Cube®

Molecuball™ and Stuff-a-Ball®

The *Molecuball*™ (available at pet supply stores and online) is one of my favorite food/treat dispensers. So named because it is shaped like—you guessed it—a molecule, this nifty device is made of durable, non-toxic thermoplastic, and has a hole at the top. The ball comes in three sizes. The size of the hole and the shape of the ball keep things challenging, but not so difficult that dogs lose interest. To ensure that dogs do not chew through the ball, it should be left with them only at mealtimes or while dispensing treats.

The Stuff-a-Ball® is an octagonal-shaped ball made of hard rubber, with one large hole. On each side are long ridges that are meant to encourage dental health. The ball can be filled with dry treats such as kibble or cookies; it dispenses the goodies easily when rolled around. The treats fall out more easily than with the other dispensers, so it might not keep dogs busy as long—then again, it stays in one piece with disembowlers like Mojo, and is good for dogs who are new to treat dispensers. The Stuff-a-Ball® comes in three sizes. My dogs love theirs, and clients appreciate the ease with which it can be filled.

Figure 1. Molecuball™
Figure 2. Stuff-a-Ball®
Figure 3. Demo by Mojo.   *Fig. 3*

Fig. 1

Fig. 2

Let's Take a Walk!

Now that we've talked about tools to provide your clients' dogs with mental stimulation, let's talk about getting them out for some physical exercise. Many dogs are not taken for walks because they pull so hard that it is an ordeal for their humans. That lack of exercise can result in a variety of behavior problems. The more you know about tools that can make walks more pleasant for everyone, the better you can serve your clients.

Front-Clip Body Harnesses

The front-clip body harness is a fairly new training innovation, and an extremely useful one. Its simple design makes it fast and easy to fit, and unlike a traditional body harness, the leash attaches to a ring that sits at the dog's chest. If the dog pulls to the end of the leash, the pressure causes him to arc back around toward the person walking him.

Dogs have an "oppositional reflex," meaning that if they are pulled in one direction, their instinct is to pull against that force. That is why, when a leash is placed on a puppy for the first time and the owner tries to tug the pup along, the pup "puts on the brakes." Any collar around a dog's neck can engage the oppositional reflex if the dog pulls. The front-clip body harness eliminates that problem.

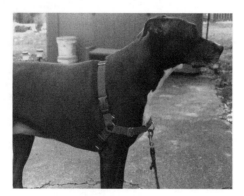

The Gentle Leader®
Easy Walk™ Harness

While a front-clip body harness will not allow you to direct a dog's head, it will give better control than a traditional body harness, and most dogs accept the harness readily. Front-clip harnesses are a good choice for dogs who pull, but are not aggressive towards other dogs or people on walks. They are also easy to put on and remove. Premier's Gentle Leader® Easy Walk™ Harness, the most popular brand, is available in bulk through the manufacturer (you can sell directly them to your clients), and in pet supply stores.

Head Halters

Head halters are a good choice for dogs who are aggressive toward other dogs or people on walks. They are also helpful when your client's dog is large or strong, and the client is small, frail or physically disabled. Head halters have been called "power steering" for dogs, and it's true. They do not allow dogs to pull with much force. Mojo weighs 120 pounds, which is more than I weigh soaking wet. He's well trained, but if he sees a cat, all bets are off. You can imagine what *that* would be like if he wore a regular collar! Using a head halter allows me enough control enough to remain standing, feet planted, and the cats, not to become hors d'oeuvres. (Yes, you can train dogs not to bolt after cats, but it happens so seldom in our case that it's not worth my training time; the head halter is good management.) Head halters eliminate any pressure on the neck, give owners the ability to direct the dog's head (helpful in situations where it is necessary to get the dog's attention quickly), and even to close the dog's mouth if necessary.

The two most common head halters are the Gentle Leader® (not to be confused with the body harness) and the Halti®. Both are made of lightweight nylon, and consist of a strap that fits over the dog's muzzle, and two straps that snap together behind the head. Neither is a "muzzle" in the traditional sense; a dog can still yawn, eat, and bark while wearing a head halter. The leash attaches to a small ring under the dog's chin. There are differences between the two brands: the Gentle Leader® has a single nylon strip around the muzzle, with a plastic clip to keep it firmly in place. The Halti® has two diagonal strips that are attached to the main muzzle strap, forming a fabric basket. Rather than the plastic clip, there is a small metal ring that causes the muzzle strip to tighten when the dog pulls. The Halti® also has a safety strap attached that clips to the dog's flat buckle collar. That way, even if the dog manages to pull out of the head halter, the leash is still attached to the buckle collar.

Above: Gentle Leader®
(These are now available in thinner muzzle strap widths as well.)

Left: Halti®

With the head halter, a short acclimation period is often necessary, since dogs do not naturally like the feel of anything over their muzzles. The brief adjustment period is worth it in the long run. Many owners of fearful or aggressive dogs find that in addition to making their dogs easier to walk, head halters have a noticeable calming effect. In fact, the manufacturer of the Gentle Leader® calls attention to the fact that pups seem to relax when their mothers pick them up by the nape of the neck, and theorize that the head halter has the same effect. Another possible explanation is that the calming effect results from the head strap pressing on a natural acupressure calming point. Whatever the reason, many dogs have an obvious relaxation response when a head halter is worn.

You should become comfortable with head halters before using them with clients' dogs. Practice fitting them properly and walking your own dogs with them first. Premier, the company that manufactures the Gentle Leader®, has a video available that shows how to properly fit and use it. Some dogs do not like the feel of any head halter at first. I explain to clients that it is like getting used to wearing glasses or a bra. At first it is uncomfortable, and is all you can think about; after a while you forget it's there. If I'm working with a couple, I usually turn to the man and say, "You remember your first bra, don't you?" (Okay, I have a feisty sense of humor. Lucky for me they always laugh.) While some dogs resist at first, most adjust to head halters quickly, especially if the halter is paired with treats and/or walks. See the product instructions for further guidance on how to help dogs acclimate to head halters, and correct usage.

Note: While it is normal for a dog to fuss a bit with a head halter during the acclimation period, a small percentage of dogs completely "shut down," lie motionless, and look miserable. For those dogs, head halters are not appropriate.

The advantages of selling head halters or body harnesses to your clients are that you can make extra income, ensure that the fit is correct and the equipment is the right choice for the dog, and you can give clients supervised practice with the equipment. It also saves your clients the trouble of going to the store. If you wish to sell Gentle Leaders® or any other Premier products (including the Gentle Leader® Easy Walk™ Harness), set up an account with the company so you can purchase them at wholesale prices. (See *Resources*.)

Martingale Collars

Martingale-style collars look similar to the regular nylon buckle collars we are all familiar with, but have an extra strip of nylon with a ring attached, which makes them operate like a limited slip collar. The leash attaches to the ring on the extra strip. When pulled, it brings the two rings on the main collar together so it tightens, but does not choke the dog. Martingales give more control than regular collars, and are especially helpful for dogs who tend to slip out of their collars, like narrow-headed sighthound breeds.

The Premier company offers martingale-style collars, sold under the name The Premier® collar; they can be ordered in bulk for resale to your clients. Or, you can refer clients to local pet supply stores to purchase martingale-style collars.

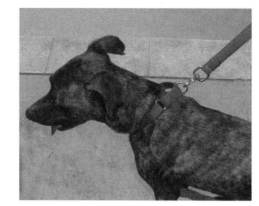

*Martingale
collar*

Clickers

Clicker training is a non-coercive, effective, fun way to train dogs. Though I do not use clickers for every training situation, there is always a supply in my toolbox.

A clicker is similar to those little tin cricket party favors. Most modern clickers consist of a metal tab inside a rectangular plastic shell. When depressed, the tab makes a clicking sound. The trainer clicks at the exact second the dog performs the correct behavior; each click is followed by a treat. (Why else would a dog care about earning a click?) For example, we might lure a dog into a down position, click at the second his body is flat on the ground, then treat. "Marking" the correct body posture or action by clicking lets the dog know the exact behavior we want. Once the dog "gets it" and is performing the desired behavior consistently, we simply give the behavior a name, that is, add a verbal cue (for example, "down") just before the behavior happens; the dog will associate the word with the behavior. Once the dog is responding consistently to the verbal cue, the clicker can be phased out.

Clicker training is often used in conjunction with food luring, but it can also be used to shape or "capture" behaviors without luring. Shaping refers to rewarding successive approximations of a behavior (breaking it down into small pieces, and rewarding and building on each one). Capturing a behavior means clicking and treating when a dog happens to do something on his own, like yawning. If clicked at that exact moment often enough, the dog will start to offer the behavior. Clicker training teaches dogs to think for themselves, and is mentally stimulating to both dogs and people.

If you are accustomed to the type of training where commands are issued, and dogs are manipulated into position and then praised, clicker training may seem odd at first—but it is worth researching and learning about. Owners are constantly amazed at how quickly their dogs learn and how well they focus with clicker training; and, to be honest, it's just a fun way to train. You will find some excellent clicker training books, videos and DVDs listed in the *Resources* section, along with sources to purchase clickers. My own clickers have my company name, logo and phone number imprinted on them. Yours should too, and should be handed out to every client you use them with.

Treats

It's a good idea to bring a few different types of treats to training sessions. After all, treat-training is difficult if the dog doesn't like your treats. If you get stuck, you could always ask the clients whether they have something on hand the dog likes—but it's better to be prepared.

Everyone has their own favorite training treat. Mine is Dick Van Patten's Natural Balance® dog food rolls. This sausage-like roll has healthy ingredients, and smells almost like beef jerky. In fact, I once had a client who left the roll in her refrigerator when she and her family went on vacation, and came back to find that their cleaning person had been making sandwiches with it! For training treats, slice the roll, then dice each coin-shaped slice into small, pea-sized squares. (Training treats should be roughly pea-sized—or a bit bigger for larger dogs—and easily chewable.)

Other popular training treats include string cheese or hot dogs cut into coin-size slices. If you don't like the greasiness of hot dogs, microwave them for thirty seconds, then cool before use.

Assess-A-Hand®

Trainer Sue Sternberg, who does incredible work with shelter dogs across the country, is responsible for a wonderful invention called the Assess-A-Hand®. This simple but brilliant tool consists of a wooden dowel covered by foam and a man's shirtsleeve, with a plastic hand at the end. Although it doesn't look exactly like a human arm, it is realistic enough that many a dog who guards food will take exception to it reaching for their dish.

I cannot emphasize strongly enough the value of the Assess-A-Hand® when testing for resource guarding. I used it once to help temperament test a Chow mix. As the dog hovered over his food, I moved the hand slowly from behind, into his peripheral vision, then toward the food. The dog not only snapped at the hand, but bit it repeatedly, chomping up the arm toward me! I have to admit that I (and the others standing around me) jumped about five feet in the air. I was thankful to have been using the Assess-A-Hand®. The product is also useful for getting leashes onto fearful or aggressive dogs, and for testing for stranger approach/aggression (to gauge whether a dog would actually bite if someone came up and petted him). See *Resources* for ordering information.

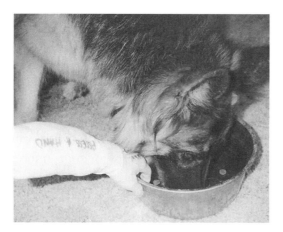

Assess-A-Hand®

Tethers

A tether is a short length (usually four to six feet) of plastic-coated wire cable. Some tethers have metal clips on both ends so one end can be clipped to the dog's collar, and the other, to an eyebolt fastened to the wall. Others have a clip at one end and a small loop at the other, so it can be anchored around the leg of a heavy piece of furniture (place the tether around the leg, then slip the clip through the loop and attach it to the dog's collar). A normal leash may be used as a tether, but many dogs will chew through leashes. (That problem can also be solved by using a taste deterrent—see the section that follows.)

The purpose of a tether is to keep a dog contained in one area. It can be used to teach dogs to settle down while their humans relax, to manage multiple dogs who are enjoying chew toys so they will not fight over them, and to help with housebreaking. (Dogs will not soil in their own little areas, and a tether drastically reduces that area.) If an owner is occupied, a destructive or non-housebroken dog could be tethered nearby to prevent unwanted behavior.

Tethers should only be used when owners are present. A dog bed should be provided, along with a stuffed Kong® or other chew toy. Order the April 2001 issue of the *Whole Dog Journal* (see in *Resources*) for instructions on how to make your own tethers, or puchase ready-made ones listed in the *Resources* section.

Taste Deterrents

Taste deterrents are normally found in spray form (they are also available as creams), and are used to prevent dogs from chewing on things we'd prefer they not chew. The sprays are typically used on furniture, but can be applied to many items. The most popular brand is Grannick's Bitter Apple®. This classic standby is effective with a large percentage of dogs. There is a small constituency, however, who consider it a delicacy and will lick it enthusiastically wherever it is sprayed. Do you have to ask? Yes, Mojo loves it. Since no brand will deter every dog anyway, it's good to have a few on hand. Pet supply stores usually stock at least two or three brands. If you keep a few in the bag you take along to appointments, you can perform a taste test with client's dogs to see which ones elicit that "yuck" response, thus saving the client money by not having them buy the wrong thing, and impressing them with how prepared you are.

Knowledge

"Knowledge" might seem like a strange thing to include in your "toolbox," but it is arguably the most valuable thing you have to offer. All the gadgets, treats and toys in the world won't mean a thing unless you understand how to use them effectively. The more solutions you have to a problem, the better. Let's say your client has a dog who is generally nervous and fearful. What's in your toolbox besides behavior modification techniques? Are you familiar with herbal remedies? Bach Flowers? Holistic remedies? Products with DAP (Dog Appeasing Pheremone)? What about Ttouch (a form of massage that is extremely effective on animals)? The more you know, the more you can offer in terms of possible solutions. (Information about the use of these products for fearful dogs can be found in the book *Help for your Fearful Dog*—see *Resources*.)

Knowledge of local resources is also important. What if a dog's behavior issue would be best addressed by burning off some energy during the day, rather than being confined to the yard alone? Are you familiar with local doggy daycare centers? What about a competent petsitter/ dogwalker? Perhaps a local agility class that dog and owner could attend would help. You don't have to learn about everything at once, but do keep your ears and mind open. Become a repository of information. Things you pick up along the way might not seem immediately useful, but there will be a time when they will come in handy.

Other things to keep in your toolbox include leashes, collars, long-lines, toys, target sticks (for clicker training), balls, bandages and other first aid supplies (just in case!), books, and handouts. You might have noticed that there are no choke chains or electronic collars in my toolbox. That's because I choose not to use them.

16

Preparation for In-Home Sessions

Phone Screening

We've already discussed general tips for taking incoming calls. Here are some specific questions that should be included in every phone screening:

1. *Dog's breed, gender, and age.* This information can give you a heads-up on possible reasons for behavior issues, and some idea of a likely prognosis. For example, terrier breeds are known diggers; Siberian Huskies can be escape artists. Finding those issues in those breeds would not be unusual. A scenario where two same-aged female dogs are fighting is not as likely to be easily resolved as one that involves a male/female fighting pair of different ages. Older dogs have been practicing behaviors longer, so will be more set in their ways than younger ones.

2. *Is the dog spay/neutered?* This can be an important factor when it comes to issues such as male-male dog-dog aggression, and male marking.

3. *Does the dog have any medical problems?* Just as people act differently when they are in pain, so do dogs. Although a medical issue causing a behavior issue is not a conclusion that should be jumped to, in cases that involve sudden onset aggression, it could well be the case. On a less dramatic note, you will want to know about medical issues so you don't, for example, recommend a strenuous exercise program for a dog with hip dysplasia. At the session, be sure to ask about food allergies as well, so you don't use treats that might cause the dog to have an allergic reaction.

4. *Are there other animals in the home?* Note their breed/age/gender, whether they have behavior issues, and how all the animals get along.

5. *Are there other adults or children in the home? Ages of children?* Having young children in the home can contribute to the implications of a behavior issue. For example, it's one thing for adults to live with a dog who guards his food, but quite another when a small child is involved. Depending on the issue, you might need to make sure the children are present for the training session.

6. *Is the client interested in teaching the dog basic obedience and manners, or is a behavior issue involved?*
   a. If obedience and manners, what specifically does the owner want to teach?
   b. If behavioral, what is the main issue? Get a brief description.

7. *Are there other behavior issues?* Sometimes this question helps to bring up things the client would not otherwise have thought to mention. For example, the call might have been prompted by the dog chewing on the table leg, but when you ask about other problems, they mention that he also lunges at people on walks.

8. *Does the dog live indoors with the family, or in the back yard?*

9. *Has the dog ever bitten or attempted to bite another animal or person? What does he do when an unfamiliar person walks in the door? How long has it been since he has met a new person?*

While some of these questions could be glossed over on the phone in favor of asking them in person, number 9 is not negotiable. *Ask about aggression even if it seems totally out of context with the issue the client is calling about.* I once had a client call with the complaint that his dog, a sweet Dalmatian/Australian Shepherd mix, had chewed numerous garden hoses and was destroying the back yard. I walked in to find Cerebus, the three-headed beast that guards the gates of hell! The 120-pound Pit Bull/Mastiff mix had the largest head and most bulging eyes I have ever seen on a dog. That the eyes pointed outward in different directions didn't help. Still, all of that would have been fine, save for his behavior. I had met the family outside and followed them into the house. They had no problem walking past Cerebus, but apparently I was not to be allowed past the entryway. As he snarled at me, saliva flying, it was apparent that not only was this dog not happy to see me, but his biggest problem did *not* involve garden hoses. I used all the calming body language possible. This dog looked at me and said in no uncertain terms, "#$*% you *and* your body language!" This boy had some major aggression issues, which should have been mentioned on the phone. The incident certainly taught me a lesson about remembering to ask whether a dog has ever threatened anyone. (I stayed for the session but honestly, at the time I probably should have referred it to another trainer. Remember, there is nothing wrong with admitting you are uncomfortable with a case, or that you don't have all the answers. Besides, that way your reputation and all your body parts will remain intact!)

After gathering phone information, if you decide to schedule an appointment, get the correct spelling of the client's name, the dog's name, address, directions, home phone, and alternate phone (cell or work number). Ask too how the caller was referred. As a courtesy—and to cut down on no-shows and last-minute cancellations—always call your clients the evening before an appointment to confirm.

Keeping Track

After the phone call, where will the data you have so diligently recorded be saved? How will you record further information at the session? It helps to have an individual sheet for each client. The form will allow you to keep track of important information, and to record what takes place at each session so you know where to pick up the next time.

On the following page is my client record sheet. Feel free to copy it. You could add a section where you circle Fair, Good or Excellent (or a scale of one to five) to rate how well a session went. You could even develop a code of notations such as DC for Difficult Client, EC for Excellent Client, and so forth (Use codes rather than writing the phrases out, in case you ever leave your notebook at a client's home!) Client sheets can be three-hole punched and kept in a loose-leaf binder. Or, you could have the form on a laptop or hand-held electronic device that you bring to sessions, then transfer the information to your home computer later on. Some trainers send out a questionnaire beforehand for the client to fill out and return with a deposit. If you do, your form should be more detailed. (*The Dog Trainer's Business Kit* CD-ROM has the latest versions of both of these forms.)

Name: _____   Date: _____
Address _____   Dog's Name: _____
       _____   Breed: _____
Phone: _____   Age/Sex: _____
E-mail: _____   Spay/Neut.? _____
Ref. by:_____

Other Pets in Household: _____
Other People in Household: _____
Occupation/Time Spent outside home: _____

Veterinarian: _____
Medical/Allergies:_____

Brand of Food: _____   How many times per day?_____
What times is dog fed? _____ Eat right away/finish? _____
Other treats/chewies & how often _____

Where was dog obtained/How long ago:_____
Housebroken? ___ Crate trained? ___ Where does dog sleep? _____
% time indoor/out? _____ Where left when alone? _____

Any previous training? Known behaviors/training methods used:
_____
_____

Exercise Type/Freq. _____
Equip. used on walks _____
Has dog ever bitten/injured person or animal? (Describe below)
_____
_____

Reason for Consultation: _____
_____
_____

Notes:
_____
_____
_____
_____
_____

Scheduling

When it comes to scheduling in-home appointments, try to stick with a workload and hours with which you are comfortable. While you are somewhat at the mercy of clients' availabilities, if you have decided that Sunday is your day to spend with your family, do not take a Sunday appointment just because a client suggests it would be more convenient. It's awfully tempting, especially when you first start out, to bend over backwards to accommodate clients. If you compromise too much, however, you will end up with appointments at odd hours, working at times when you are not at your best. Strive for a comfortable balance.

As your business grows, scheduling and setting boundaries will become even more important. Some trainers are comfortable doing two to three in-home appointments daily, while others prefer to do five or six. You will develop a feel for what you can handle, and how much time to leave between appointments for travel. If you schedule an unusually heavy day or two, try to make the next day light or completely free. Of course, some trainers prefer to spread appointments out more evenly. If, for example, you are at your most energetic and ready to work in the mornings, but are lethargic by 4:00 p.m., you might want to spread your appointments out over as many mornings as possible, then have the rest of your days free.

Obvious though it may sound, it is important to maintain a good energy level and to stay healthy. If you have scheduled a few appointments in a row, bring along a cooler with snacks like string cheese or yogurt to keep your hunger down and blood sugar steady. Coolers also come in handy for keeping extra dog treats fresh.

Exercise or do other stress-relieving activities that you enjoy. Take short vacations to recharge your batteries. Every job, no matter how enjoyable, carries the potential for burnout. Dog training can contribute not only to physical stress, but to mental stress, especially if you handle serious behavior issues. Setting guidelines and limits from the beginning, sticking to them, and taking good care of your mind and body will go a long way toward ensuring a long and rewarding career.

17

The Appointment

What Do I Do Now?

The time arrives for your appointment. Naturally, you are prompt, presentable, and ready to work. Now what? You have just a few seconds to make a good first impression, so be friendly and professional. Smile and introduce yourself. As you do, take note of the dog's behavior. (If the case involves human-directed aggression, you should have previously arranged to have the dog outside or otherwise managed for your arrival.) You can obtain vital information by simply observing the dog as you speak with the owner, both at the door and as you sit and chat. Notice the owner's interactions with the dog as well.

Spend as much time as necessary to get all the pertinent details regarding the issues that were mentioned during the phone screening. You may also notice things in the environment that prompt you to ask further questions. A good trainer is part detective. Often the piece of information that solves a behavioral puzzle is something you must notice or ferret out, rather than relying on the client to offer it.

Once you have interviewed the client, you should have a solid idea of the issues to be addressed. If the focus is on obedience training and manners, you will know which skills need to be taught. Be sure to ask directly about the client's overall goals for the dog as well. If, for example, the dog is an outdoor dog who is being destructive, is the client's goal solely to have the dog stop chewing the garden hose and destroying the flower beds? Or is there a larger goal of wanting the dog to become an indoor dog who can be trustworthy in the house?

It is crucial to know what your clients want. What *you* think is best for their dogs may differ at times; that is one of the challenges of this profession. All you can do is give the client the facts, along with your expert advice. It's tough not to blurt things like, "Why did you get a dog if it's going to be in the back yard alone all day?" Unfortunately, that would not only be unprofessional, it would alienate the client. Remember that saying about catching more flies with honey than with vinegar? It's true. You will get further with clients by nicely pointing out why spanking the dog isn't really effective, and by offering alternatives, than you will by blaming or berating them. And in the end, you'll be helping the dog.

Ten Tips for In-Home Sessions

The specifics of how to teach basic obedience skills and address behavior issues is beyond the scope of this book. However, many of the books in the *Resources* section contain excellent information on those subjects. Regardless of which issues are involved, here are ten tips that will help at any in-home training session:

1. *Minimize distractions.* Recommend to your client in advance to let the answering machine pick up calls during the session. If there are other pets in the household, suggest they be placed in another room with a yummy chew toy while training takes place. Young children should be provided with an activity like coloring or watching a DVD. Without those preparations, you might find yourself interrupted constantly, which can make training difficult, if not impossible.

2. *Don't assume that the information the client provides is accurate.* What the client tells you is her perception of the dog's behavior, but you will get more information by keeping your eyes and ears open, and observing the dog's behavior and dog-owner interactions. Note what the client says, but don't take it as gospel. The dog will give you the real story.

3. *Be patient with the dog.* Let fearful dogs come to you; don't pressure or coerce them. Constantly monitor the dog's reactions to your actions, and don't push training to the point where the dog is getting stressed or frustrated. Remember that young pups in particular have very short

attention spans. It's fine to take short breaks during which you discuss things with the client. Let the dog's behavior dictate your rate of progress.

4. *Be patient with the owner.* As previously mentioned, most of dog training is really about training the owners. Try not to get frustrated when someone doesn't understand a concept or can't perform an exercise. Break things into small, achievable steps for them, just as you do for dogs. As trainer extraordinaire Bob Bailey says, "Training is a mechanical skill." When someone is first trying to juggle a clicker, treats and leash, it's difficult! Be supportive and make things easier whenever necessary. It can help to remind clients that when they first learned to drive, it was hard to concentrate on doing so many things at once. Training, like driving, becomes fluent and natural with practice. And remember, it's important to give owners positive reinforcement when they do something correctly!

> It is good practice for you, being a teacher, to learn a new skill once in a while. I recently enrolled in a bellydancing class. Trust me, coordinating all those isolated movements is not easy, and I found myself with a whole new empathy for those clicker-leash-treat juggling clients!

5. *Stay focused.* Refrain from telling long, involved stories about your own dogs or your training experiences. While a brief mention of something personal and relevant can be useful, a long, drawn-out account of your personal adventures might well cause clients to wonder why they're paying by the hour to listen to it. Be sure to cover the main issues you came to address. If you feel there are other issues that need attention, say so, and schedule another session if necessary.

6. *Show, don't tell.* If you expect a client to carry out a program, don't just hand over a protocol and expect that it will be followed. Instructions on paper aren't always perceived in the way they were intended, and besides, most people learn better by practicing hands-on. Show clients exactly what you want them to do with their dogs, step by step, then have them practice so you can give feedback. Should the dog not react in the expected way, you can modify the exercise as needed.

7. *Offer a few possible solutions.* There is always more than one solution to a problem, and it is important that you come up with one that is feasible for the client. Even the best solution is worthless if it does not fit in with a client's lifestyle, capabilities or commitment to carry it out. Keep programs simple and realistic, and give specific instructions on what to do and how and when to progress to the next level. For behavior modification issues, you will need to give specific instructions each week, as well as giving an overview of the program at the start. That way the client won't get overwhelmed, can stay on track, and you can modify the program as needed.

8. *Don't take failures personally.* It is inevitable that at some point, a training exercise you are attempting will not work. (Hey, sometimes the dogs just haven't read the right training books!) If that happens, simply take a moment to analyze the situation, then come up with another way of tackling the problem. You might need to break the behavior down into smaller steps for the dog to understand. Or, you could switch to another approach altogether. The ability to revise your approach on the fly is part of the art of being a good trainer, and will develop as you gain experience. You will also find that programs sometimes fail because owners don't comply with your instructions. That does not mean you have failed. Know that you did the best you could, and that sometimes things are out of your hands.

9. *Just say "No."* If it becomes clear that an issue is not what was represented to you on the phone and is not something you are comfortable working with, say so. Again, there is nothing wrong with bowing out gracefully and referring the client to another trainer.

10. *Reality check, please!* Most owners love and want what's best for their dogs, but unfortunately, some do not have a firm grasp of what is possible in the realm of canine behavior. It is inevitable that you will come across owners who have unrealistic expectations. It is sometimes difficult for novice trainers (and even experienced ones) to tell owners that the behavior they want from the dog is simply not going to happen. After all, we all want to please our clients and feel that we can help them to accomplish their goals. However, it is important to draw the line between high expectations and unreality, and to develop a knack for telling owners when their expectations are simply unrealistic. Expecting a dog to

urinate in a specific spot in the yard is realistic, so long as the owner is willing to leash the dog and lead him to that spot repeatedly at the start. Expecting an unsupervised, unneutered male dog to stop marking over the spot where another dog keeps urinating is unrealistic. Whenever possible, strive to reach a compromise where the owner still gets what she wants and the dog is set up to succeed. If that is not possible, tell the owner in a nice way that what she wants is simply unrealistic to expect of *any* dog.

The Wrap-Up

Your session has gone well and now it's time to depart. Leave your clients with business cards and any applicable handouts. Be sure they understand how to proceed with the training program, and if warranted, schedule another appointment. If another appointment is not necessary, you could ask the clients to call you in a week or two to let you know how things are progressing. Or, say you will call them. Follow-up calls are a good way to gauge the success of the programs you prescribe, and offer an opportunity to help iron out any snags that may have arisen. They also offer an opportunity to schedule another appointment if necessary. And, following up shows your concern.

Just after you leave the session, record any extra notes or thoughts. It is all too easy to forget exactly what was accomplished, or what you plan to do at the next session, if you wait too long.

A Few Final Considerations

While these considerations do not apply to the actual visit, they are important for any trainer who does in-home training:

• Well-meaning acquaintances or clients may have a friend who is interested in training. They may ask that you give the person a call. *Don't do it.* People who are not motivated enough to call you themselves have a low likelihood of following through with a training program. Thank the person for the referral, and ask that the friend call you directly.

• If you arrive at an appointment but the client is nowhere to be found, wait. Traffic jams and other delays are inevitable. If the client still has not shown up after fifteen minutes, leave a pleasant note on the door stating that you were there for the appointment, that you hope everything is alright, and to please call you to reschedule. You could even have the notes pre-printed. As annoyed as you might be, do not leave an angry note; who knows, there might have been a real emergency. Besides, even if you have a cancellation clause in your contract, it will be difficult to collect your fee if the client is offended. When the client calls to reschedule, be gracious. If there is a cancellation fee involved, remind the person that it will be due at the next appointment.

• See aggression cases as the first appointment of your day, or whenever you are at your most alert and clear-thinking. Do *not* see aggression cases if you have not slept the night before or are otherwise "out of it." It is better to reschedule than to make a serious error in judgment. (For more on handling aggression cases, see *Resources* for *Getting a Grip on Aggression Cases*.)

• Sooner or later, you will come across a client who just won't let you go. You have helped with the initial concerns and maybe a few others, and the dog is doing fabulously. The client, however, has become attached to your weekly visits. The reason may be anything from a lack of confidence to continue the training on her own, to loneliness, to simply enjoying your company. While continuing the training might be beneficial to your finances, the ethical course is to let the person know you have completed the training that was agreed upon, and that you feel she is fully capable of continuing on her own. Should she say that she would feel better training for a few more weeks with your assistance, or there are other things to work on, fine. So long as the client is still getting something out of the training sessions, and you are willing to continue, go for it. But if you find that the client is just hanging on without any real justification, the ethical thing to do is to gently disengage.

18

Group Class Considerations

Types of Classes

There are various types of group classes, the most common being basic obedience for adult dogs. Some trainers also offer intermediate and advanced classes. For puppies, there are "kindergarten" groups which focus on socialization, puppy issues and some basic obedience. Some classes specifically offer clicker training. A clicker training class usually includes basic obedience, along with other clicker-friendly options such as targeting (teaching dogs to touch a target with nose or paw) and shaping behaviors.

A more specialized type of class is a "growl class," which focuses on dogs who are reactive/aggressive with other dogs. Although growl classes are becoming more popular, they are not something a novice instructor should attempt. A great option for a class that a novice/intermediate trainer could teach, however, is a tricks class. This type of class can be taught with or without clickers, and may be one of the most fun groups you will ever teach. People have a light-hearted attitude while teaching tricks; they and their dogs end up having a great time while they learn. Strive to infuse even your basic obedience classes with that light-hearted, fun atmosphere. After all, those obedience skills are all just tricks to the dogs!

Location

First, you'll need a training space. Some trainers are lucky enough to have their own indoor facility. While you probably won't start out that way, if there is space available within a local pet supply store, for example, ask whether it can be rented by the hour. Other indoor spaces to check into are school gymnasiums, groomer's shops, veterinary offices, veterans halls, dance or martial arts studios, or community recreation rooms. Outdoor options include parks, parking lots (try pet supply stores, churches, or even funeral homes), or school grounds. If you plan to teach a puppy class, you will need a safe space where the pups are not in danger of contracting diseases. As previously mentioned, a public park is not an appropriate place to hold a puppy class.

How Many Students?

Once you have space reserved, you'll still have a few decisions to make. First, how many dogs will be allowed in each class? The number will depend on how much space you have to work in, whether you work alone or with assistants, what you are comfortable with, and what is financially feasible. Although there is obviously more money to be made with larger classes, there is also less personal attention given (unless you have assistants), which can be frustrating to both you and the owners. You will probably start out by teaching on your own, so keep your class size manageable. As mentioned, six dogs to one instructor should be the limit. That way you can give personal attention to each dog/owner team and keep track of what is going on in the environment. You could even, as previously referenced, offer very small classes, marketing them as exclusive, "semi-private" groups, and accept only two to four students.

Fees

Once you have decided how many dogs to enroll, set your fees. Call around to see what the going rate is in your area. Calculate fees based on the minimum number of dogs you will accept in class, so that if you don't have the maximum, it will still be worth your while financially.

Scheduling

Schedule your classes at times that are convenient for the general public. Weekday evenings are popular, as are weekend mornings, late afternoons, and early evenings. In the summer, avoid scheduling classes during the middle of the day; the heat can make things uncomfortable and potentially dangerous for both dogs and people. (If you can't avoid the heat, suggest that students bring water for their dogs and themselves, along with sunscreen.) If you're working indoors, of course, you won't have to worry about the weather or having enough light. Set evening classes late enough to give people time to get home from work, but not so late that people won't be motivated to come. Evening classes usually start around 7:00-7:30 p.m. and, like most classes, last an hour.

How Many Classes?

A basic obedience course for adult dogs usually lasts somewhere between six and ten weeks, with classes meeting once a week. Some trainers prefer that dogs not be present at the first class. That way, owners can pay attention without worrying about what their dogs are doing, and can participate in people-oriented teaching games and exercises. Other trainers feel that owners get more out of classes if dogs are present from the beginning. If you are doing a specialized class such as a tricks class, you could opt for a less traditional structure, such as three or four two-hour sessions.

Advertising

Once you have classes scheduled, it's time to let people know about them. If you are offering classes through a Parks Department, they will probably advertise for you. If your classes will be held at a vet's office or through a pet supply store, with their permission, leave a sign-up sheet on the premises. You can then call those who have left their numbers to give them more information. You might also post flyers around town, and advertise the class in local publications. Class information should be included on your website as well. Be sure to emphasize what's special about your class. For example, let people know that it's a clicker training class, or that they'll be playing games, and that it's a fun and effective way for them and their dogs to learn.

Phone Screening

When you phone prospective students, be sure to review the class date and time, fees, and (in general terms) what the class will cover. Inform them of any specific policies, for example, the minimum age for children to be allowed to attend. Some trainers allow children ages eight and over, and do not let children under the age of eighteen attend without a parent. Explain your requirements for the dogs' vaccination status as well. For a puppy class, some trainers accept those who have had at least two (or three, depending on the trainer) rounds of vaccinations, while others want the dogs to be fully vaccinated. Some trainers will accept titers instead (titers measure antibodies through a blood test).

Be sure to ask prospective group class students this very important question: *Has your dog ever bitten or attempted to bite another dog or person?* Phrase it that way, rather than asking, "Is your dog aggressive?" The definition of "aggressive" varies from one dog owner to the next. It is crucial that you have this information ahead of time, as it would be quite unpleasant for class members (and you!) to be surprised by a dog-aggressive or people-aggressive dog in their midst. Including a seriously aggressive dog in class is not only an unfair imposition on your students and their dogs, but is a potential liability. Suggest private behavior modification sessions for aggressive dogs instead.

While a seriously dog-aggressive dog has no place in an average group class, if you are comfortable with the idea and have the space, you could accept dogs who are simply "reactive" with other dogs. In other words, they might bark and lunge at other dogs, but it is fear-based. It's the dog's way of saying, "Stay away from me, you big scary thing!" Most reactive dogs I have accepted into class were either afraid or were bullies, technically more "dog-obnoxious" than dog-aggressive.

If you choose to accept dog-reactive dogs in your classes, do not allow more than one (or two at the most) in any given class. Inform owners at the start that the dog is not seriously aggressive and is no threat to their dogs, but it would be appreciated if everyone could help by letting him have his space. Have the dog and owner work at a comfortable distance from the other dogs, and gradually move closer as progress is made. In almost all the cases I have encountered, the reactive dog was able to work in much closer to the other dogs by the end of the last class. And, even if the reactive dog was too stressed to completely absorb the training, if he simply learned to be more comfortable around other dogs, it was beneficial.

Form Letters/Contracts

Once you have established that a dog is a good candidate for class, get the owner's address and send a form letter. The letter should cover where and when the class will be held, the fee, what to bring (for example, treats, vaccination records) and class rules. Along with the letter, include a contract that releases you and the provider of your teaching space from liability, should a mishap occur. Ask that the contract be signed and returned with payment in order to guarantee a place in class. Getting payment in advance is an invaluable practice. That way you will know for certain how many people will be attending, and can avoid giving a class for only a few people, or having too many to manage.

Following is a sample form letter for a puppy class:

Congratulations on choosing to train your puppy using dog-friendly, people-friendly, positive methods!

The class you are enrolling in will provide plenty of playtime/socialization with other pups. We will discuss solutions to common problems such as nipping, chewing, jumping up on people, and more. Your pup will also get an introduction to sitting, lying down, and coming when called. You will learn about canine behavior and body language, and how dogs think and learn.

Please bring: *Location*:   *ABC Veterinary Clinic*
- Current vaccination records   *832 Main Ave.*
- Your pup, wearing a plain collar   *ph: 555-0672*
  (no choke chains or retractable leashes)
- Treats such as hot dogs, cheese, freeze-dried liver, or Natural Balance roll, cut into pea or coin-sized pieces. If your pup has weight or health issues, use his regular dry food; put it in a sealed plastic bag overnight with chicken or hot dog. In the morning, remove the chicken/hot dog. The kibble will have absorbed the yummy chicken/hot dog flavor!

Enter the training area with your pup on leash, and do not approach other pups. A supervised, safe introduction is always best. All family members are welcome, including children eight years of age and over, with a parent present.

Please sign and return the enclosed Training Services Agreement, along with payment ($75) to guarantee your spot in class. Class begins Monday, May 15th at 7:30 p.m., and runs for six Mondays. Please save this letter for class location, date and time. I will phone you before the start date to touch base and answer any last-minute questions. I look forward to having you and Sadie in class!

DOG TRAINING SERVICES AGREEMENT

Dog's Name:	Owner's Name:
Breed:	Home Phone:
Age: Sex: Weight:	Work/Cell Phone:
Spay/Neutered?	Address:
Vaccinations current?	City/State/Zip:
Vet's Name:	Vet's Phone:

Training Fee:	$75.00	Start Date: Mon. May. 15, 2006	
Duration:	4 weeks	Location: ABC VeterinaryClinic	
Time:	7:30 - 8:30	832 Main Avenue ph. 800-555-0672	

First class is people only, no dogs. Please bring your dog's vaccination records.
Classes are filled on a first-come, first-served basis. A spot will not be held until payment is received, along with a signed Training Agreement. These items must be received prior to commencement of first class.

SERVICES PROVIDED: Classes are taught by Nicole Wilde ("Trainer"), a professional dog trainer. Classes are limited to 6 dogs so personal attention may be given to each dog/handler team. Trainer, at her discretion, may refuse entry to a pet which is not healthy, is aggressive, or does not seem suitable for the services provided.

PAYMENT: Payment is due prior to the start of training. No refunds will be given.

REMOVAL FROM TRAINING: Trainer, at her sole discretion, may remove a pet from class if a hazard or threat of any nature to any other animal or person is present. No refund will be given under such circumstances.

DANGER: Owner agrees to indemnify and hold ABC Vet and all Staff ("Location") and Trainer harmless from all liability for any loss, damage or injury to persons, animals or property arising from or related to Owner's pet. Owner agrees that Location and/or Trainer shall not be liable for loss or damage to animal for any reason unless said loss or damage was a direct result of Location or Trainer's negligence.

ARBITRATION: Any controversy between the parties involving any of the terms, covenants, or conditions of this Agreement shall be submitted to arbitration in Los Angeles County, California, on the request of any party, and shall comply with and be governed by the provisions of the American Arbitration Association. All decisions shall be final and binding. In any dispute between the parties, whether or not resulting in litigation, the party substantially prevailing shall be entitled to recover from the other party all reasonable costs, including without limitation, attorney's fees.

SIGNATURE/DATE: _____ ("Owner") _____ ("Trainer")

19

The Group Class

Lesson Plans

Regardless of what type of class you teach, you will need plans that outline what will be covered during each lesson. Make a list of the behaviors you want to teach during the course. For example, a basic obedience class usually covers sit, down (lie down), heel (or the less formal "loose-leash walking"), come (also known as the "recall"), and stay. Most trainers also teach attention exercises. After all, if you don't have the dog's attention, you're not going to get much of a response to anything else! In addition, some trainers include "leave it," that is, "That thing you were about to put in your mouth—don't even think about it!" and "settle" (lie down and relax). These are just the basics. You will round out your syllabus with other topics, games, and exercises related to the behaviors being taught.

The First Class

The first day of class is a good time to review procedures. Discuss protocols for dog-dog interactions, asking questions, and anything else you think is important for your students to know. The first session is also the time to check vaccination records, collars (for correct fit and type), and to collect any contracts or monies due.

Most group classes for adult dogs do not include playtime or socialization periods, but if the dogs are friendly and the owners would like, you can certainly allow the dogs to mingle on-leash before or after class. That dogs are not allowed to mingle during class is important for owners to know before the dogs ever arrive on the scene. If your first class is for people only, that won't be a problem. If you have dogs present at the first class, outline dog-dog interaction rules in your form letter and remind owners of them by telephone before the first day of class. Naturally, you will have to remind students of the rules at times during classes as well.

As far as students asking questions during class, if they pertain to the exercise or topic at hand, address them. After all, there are no stupid questions, and someone else is probably wondering the same thing. More individualized questions can be raised during the fifteen minute pre-class setup time, or for fifteen minutes afterward. If you prefer not to answer questions before or after class, you could ask students to phone you with questions during the week, or, designate the last ten minutes of your classes as question and answer periods. (A trainer I know has a ten-minute brainstorming session at the end of each class. A student poses a training or behavior question, then the instructor and the other students offer answers. This is an excellent way for students to stay involved, and many students come up with excellent, creative solutions.)

It is standard protocol for students to introduce themselves and their dogs at the first class. Remember to introduce yourself as well. In my classes, each owner was asked to give her name, the dog's name, breed and age, and to share one thing she really likes about her dog. That last bit can be very revealing. You will often get a foreshadowing of things to come when someone answers, "I can't really think of anything" or, "Oh, there are so many things, I couldn't possibly list them!" or even, "I like that she matches my couch." (And yes, I have actually heard that one!)

The first class is also the perfect time (especially if dogs are not present) to briefly explain the basic principles of dog training and psychology, and how they apply to the training you will be doing. You could include an overview of how dogs think and learn, how and when to reinforce behaviors, the importance of good timing, and so on. Your explanations should be free of scientific jargon. For example, if you want your students to switch from giving treats every time their dogs sit to treating randomly every couple of times, say so, instead of announcing that they are switching "from a continuous reinforcement schedule to one of random ratio, intermittent reinforcement." Otherwise, you'll end up with a room full of glazed expressions—and I don't mean the dogs.

If dogs are not present and you are teaching clicker training, the first class is an excellent time to let owners practice with the clicker. Students can break into pairs where one plays the dog and one the owner; the owner clicks and treats for simple behaviors like making eye contact. (People really get into this game—some even start barking and scratching!) Or, students can do exercises that will improve their timing, such as you dropping a ball and asking them to click before it hits the ground. Many clicker trainers play the "Training Game" during the first class. One student is sent from the room, while the others decide on a simple task she must perform, such as picking up a specific object. The student returns. Each time she moves in the direction that will ultimately accomplish the task, the other students click. The game teaches owners the valuable skill of shaping a behavior by breaking it down into small steps. (For a more in-depth description of this game, see *Resources* for Karen Pryor's *Don't Shoot the Dog*.) Have I mentioned how much fun everyone has playing this game? It's a hoot!

Note: If you choose to have dogs present at the first class, tell owners to reward any time their dogs are calm or make eye contact. Rewarding calm and eye contact really cuts down on first-night chaos.

Lesson Progression

When planning your courses, keep in mind that there should be a natural progression of behaviors. For example, the first thing I taught in basic obedience classes was attention. Once the dogs were more focused on their owners, the owners could teach them to sit. Down was taught after sit, because down was taught from a sitting position. Keep in mind that some behaviors, like sit and down, can be taught fairly quickly. Others, like getting a solid recall, a long stay, or walking nicely on leash are more of a process. So although sit and down are introduced almost immediately, you should introduce the other behaviors early in the curriculum as well. The goal is to introduce each behavior, then build on it. Get students to practice each behavior at home with no distractions first, then in different areas of the house, then outdoors with no distractions, and finally, teach them to "proof" the behaviors with distractions in and out of class.

You will find that you are constantly modifying your lesson plans based on the specific dogs and people in that class, the pace they can handle, and how much time is taken up by questions. Try to stick with your lesson plan, but don't get upset if you find yourself straying from it, or not getting around to minor things you wanted to include. That's the nature of the beast. With experience, you will become adept at modifying your plan on the fly so that it all comes together regardless.

Following is an example of what a single behavior might look like throughout your course. In this example, down-stay is introduced in Class Three. We will assume that the dogs have already learned sit and down. This is not an explanation of exactly how a behavior is taught, but rather, how it progresses:

Class Three: Dogs are in down position. Owners stand next to dogs. Dogs are rewarded for three-to-five-second down-stays. If a dog cannot manage three seconds, the owner begins with whatever duration the dog can handle. Owners are instructed on how to work with their dogs at home, adding time very gradually, without moving away from the dog. The goal is to have the dog do a one-minute down-stay next to the owner.

Class Four: Assuming the dogs can now down-stay with the owners next to them for a minute, the owners take one step away. The dogs down-stay for ten seconds (or, if unable, whatever they are capable of). Instruct owners on how to build distance gradually, that is, each time they add a step away, to drop back down to a ten-second stay (or less if necessary), then build duration gradually. The goal is to get three steps away from the dog during the weekly home practice.

Class Five: As the dogs remain in down-stays, owners are to introduce small distractions at close range, such as walking around the dogs, bending to tie a shoelace, doing a jumping-jack, bouncing a ball, or squeaking a toy. Owners should continue to build duration at a distance.

Class Six: Bigger distractions are introduced. While owners remain close to their dogs, a dog/owner team walks by at a distance. Also, while owners are a few steps away from their dogs, another person walks slowly in-between, or comes up to shake the owner's hand.

Class Seven: While dogs down-stay with owners at a distance, an adult student or child runs past. In another exercise, half the students practice recalls while the other half keep their dogs in down-stays.

Class Eight: Graduation! Games are played that make use of the dogs' excellent down-stays. For example, all the dogs down-stay in a line, at a distance from each other. One dog-owner team weaves through the line, with the dog in heel position. They pair place themselves at the end of the line, and the next dog/owner team repeats the exercise. This can be done as a relay race with owners broken into two teams, with penalties for dogs breaking down-stays. Don't forget prizes for the winning team!

This plan is only one example, for one exercise. You will find what works best by trying different things and modifying them, over and over. Just remember that the goal is to build on each behavior as the class progresses, so that by the last class, the dogs can perform the behaviors even with distractions. No one expects a novice class to end up with dogs who are "bomb-proof" (won't react no matter what the distraction), but aim for the best results the dogs and owners in your class are capable of.

Homework

Along with lesson plans, you will need to prepare homework assignments. Keep them short and simple. Review how to train the behavior, and give helpful tips and specifics on how to proceed. For example, rather than saying, "Practice sit this week," you might suggest that once the dog has mastered sit, the owner should ask the dog to sit before meals, and before having the leash put on for walks; to practice with the dog sitting by the owner's side, rather than facing her; and to practice sit with the owner sitting as well. Some trainers hand out a checklist to help owners keep track of their progress. Homework sheets are also an appropriate place to include any lecture material that is important, but would have taken up valuable class time (and probably not have been fully absorbed). Lecture material might include information about behavior issues, leadership, basic training principles, or health concerns, for example.

Graduation

It is great fun to have a graduation party at the last class. After all, everyone has been training diligently for the past few months. They deserve it! Graduation Day is the time to point out how far the dogs and owners have come, and to let them show off. Play games (with fun prizes) that incorporate what has been learned. Graduation certificates should be handed out, along with a small parting gift for each student/dog team. The atmosphere should be one of light-hearted celebration.

There is a wonderful game called *My Dog Can Do That* (see *Resources*), which is sure to provide fun and laughter at graduation. The game consists of a deck of cards, each of which has a task the owner/dog team must perform in order to advance. The cards are conveniently broken into beginner and more advanced tasks, so you can use those which are appropriate to your group. I cannot express the rollicking good times my students have had playing it. It is so satisfying to see a student draw a card, say "No way, my dog won't be able to do this," then watch as the dog *does* do it. Students inevitably find their dogs capable of much more than they thought! Other fun games to play at graduation include relay races and Musical Chairs. (For Musical Chairs, play as you would for people, but don't let owners take a seat until their dogs are sitting. Mats or hula hoops may be substituted for the *dogs* to sit on/in.) Terry Ryan's booklets (see *Resources*) include other great games that can be played in class.

Graduation certificates can be printed on certificate paper (available at any office supply store) using your home computer. Gold foil stickers add a nice touch. Software programs are available that include templates for certificates, or you can make your own template using a word processing program. Students really enjoy being presented with graduation certificates. I have known quite a few who have framed and hung them on their walls.

Along with the certificate, it's nice to have a small giveaway item. I really like *Bark Bars*, which are cookies shaped like cats and postmen. They come in cute bags, are cost-effective, get a laugh, and are healthy for the dogs. (Use Google to find them online.) Many trainers make their own gift bags, which include dog treats, clickers, toys, or discount coupons on products or classes. Be creative!

Saying Goodbye

At the last class, be sure to mention any upcoming classes you have scheduled, as many students will want to go on to the next level. If you do not offer next-level classes, if possible, have a referral ready to a trainer in your area who does. If you do in-home training, now is the time to remind owners they can always contact you for individual help. Be sure everyone has your business card. If you have personalized refrigerator magnets or other promotional items, distribute them. That way, students always have your number handy, and you stay in their minds for future training and referrals.

Class dismissed!

20

Puppy Kindergarten

While many of the same considerations apply regardless of which types of classes you offer, there are some that are specific to puppy class, also known as Puppy Kindergarten.

Safety First

When it comes to young pups, safety must be your priority. Owners have a legitimate concern about their puppies contracting parvo or distemper by walking or playing in an area where infected dogs have been. For that reason, most puppy classes are held indoors, in an area that has been thoroughly disinfected beforehand. Other safety considerations include making sure flooring surfaces are such that pups won't slide and injure themselves, and that there are no sharp objects or obstacles pups could run into.

As mentioned, many vets recommend that puppies not be exposed to other dogs until vaccinations are complete (at sixteen weeks, when the rabies vaccination is given). However, many trainers offer classes to pups as young as ten weeks, as long as they have had at least two rounds of vaccinations and are in good health. The period of development during which socialization has the optimum effect ends at approximately twelve weeks. That does not mean pups cannot be socialized after that, but that it is most effective to do so during that period. It is up to you and whoever owns the space you train in as to the minimum acceptable age, but remember this: *More dogs lose their lives—are surrendered to shelters for behavioral reasons and wind up euthanized—as a result of not having been socialized and trained early on, than from contracting a disease.*

If you choose to accept very young pups in class, establish a maximum age as well so that you do not end up with very young puppies being overwhelmed by much older or larger ones. My own classes were open to pups three to five months old, who had at least two rounds of vaccinations and were in good health. (The minimum age was based on the preference of the veterinarian in whose clinic I taught.) Some trainers prefer to offer classes for pups ten weeks to four months of age.

Some trainers accept pups of any size in class, as long as they are of the appropriate age, then separate them to play, using a puppy pen for smaller breeds. I recommend keeping pups on leash until specific owners are instructed to turn their pups loose to interact (usually only two to three puppies at a time). That way, you can monitor the pups' interactions, and give a running narration about body language, vocalizations, and other things of which your students should be aware. By allowing only a few pups to interact at once, you are also ensuring everyone's safety, and making sure none of the pups get overwhelmed. (This arrangement is conducive to the owners feeling calmer as well.) I believe that having a mix of sizes in class is actually preferable. Of course you wouldn't pair a Great Dane pup with a Toy Poodle pup to play, but smaller dogs should learn to play nicely with larger dogs, and vice-versa.

Once students have signed up for your class, learn a bit about each breed that is enrolled. Familiarize yourself with what each was originally bred for and what their tendencies are, so you can relate it to the training. For example, someone who has a retriever mix might have more of an issue with exuberant jumping than someone with, say, a Shiba Inu. When the owners of the Australian Shepherd ask why their pup chases their son when he walks away from the rest of the family, you could explain about the herding instinct. It is also helpful to be able to point out the differing play styles of various breeds. Being well-informed about breed characteristics when students introduce themselves and their pups, you could offer comments on each dog. For example, "Did you know that well-bred Pit Bulls are very stable and are actually excellent with children? They really have gotten a bad rap!" or "Did you know that a Rhodesian Ridgeback can bring down a lion single-handedly?" ...Okay, that one might not be so useful in everyday suburbia, but it's an interesting fact, and you'll look very knowledgeable!

Curriculum

While a Puppy Kindergarten class might offer some basic obedience training, it should also address puppy-specific issues, and include plenty of time for socialization with other pups and people. It's great when kids attend puppy classes with their parents, as it gives the other pups in class positive exposure to kids as well as adults.

Some trainers include introductory levels of obedience exercises in class, such as attention, sit, down, the recall, leave it (especially helpful for puppies), drop it—as opposed to leave it, drop it is applicable once the pup has already absconded with the item—settle, and go to bed. Depending on the available space, an introduction to loose leash walking might also be included. Some trainers choose to break classes into Puppy Level 1 and Puppy Level 2, with the first having more emphasis on socialization and common puppy behavior issues, and the second, more emphasis on obedience skills.

Regardless of how you structure your class, behavior issues and topics that should be addressed include housebreaking and crate training, jumping up, nipping/mouthiness, appropriate chew toys, periods of canine social development, items that are potentially hazardous to pups (including poisonous plants and foods such as chocolate), barking and other attention-seeking behaviors, and how to establish leadership, socialize the pups outside of class, prevent destruction in the home, and prevent separation anxiety. You should also practice handling exercises in class, so the pups become accustomed to being picked up, held, and having various parts of their bodies touched. "Pass the puppy" is a favorite class exercise, where everyone, on the instructor's cue, passes their puppy to the person on their right. The game ensures that the pups get used to being handled by a variety of people, and will prepare them for visits to the groomer and veterinarian.

Decide on the length of your course, and plan your curriculum accordingly. Most puppy classes run six to eight sessions. Mine were somewhat unusual in that they ran for only four sessions, and focused mainly on socialization, handling exercises, puppy issues and some introductory obedience exercises. Owners then had the option of enrolling the pups in my basic obedience class. Alternately, you could offer a six-to-eight week puppy class that includes all the basic obedience exercises, then let them graduate to an intermediate obedience class.

Be sure to touch base with owners before the first class begins. Remind them to bring vaccination records, treats and anything else that is required. Many trainers also ask owners to bring mats or beds for their pups. This gives each pup a specific space, and is useful in teaching "Go to your bed." Some trainers ask owners to bring their pup's favorite toy, to keep them occupied when necessary. Try different strategies and stick with what works best for you.

Rules for Playtime

It is especially important in puppy class to discuss rules for interaction, both human and canine. Will pups be on leash or off? Are pups allowed to sniff and check each other out at any time during class? What if someone's pup lunges at another? Should the owners pet other pups? In my own classes, owners were instructed to keep pups on leash, close to them, until instructed otherwise. Owners were instructed not to pet (and thereby reward) any pup who wandered over and jumped up on them.

As the pups play, you should not only comment on their body language and point out stress signals, but urge owners to do the same; in that way you can dispell misconceptions. For example, an owner might comment that the growls and barks that accompany play are a sign of aggression. They are quite relieved when you point out that these vocalizations are completely normal in the course of play.

Of course, when a pup displays truly inappropriate play behavior, you should calmly break up the interaction and have the owners put the pups back on leash to calm down. Then explain to the class what happened and why. As the course progresses, you may feel comfortable allowing more pups off-leash at once, until they are finally all playing together off-leash. This should only be done if you have a small enough class size that you can monitor all interactions.

Suggested rules of interaction for Puppy Kindergarten:

1. No pups off-leash unless you give the word.

2. When pups are off-leash, if any owner is uncomfortable with what is happening, the person may yell, "Grab your dogs!" and everyone must calmly retrieve their pups. This offers nervous owners a sense of security about the safety of their pups.

3. Don't allow any pup to become cornered; he could become defensive and bite in that situation. "Being cornered" does not apply only to physical corners, but could mean the pup is hiding behind the seated owner's legs.

4. If two pups are playing and one seems to be getting overwhelmed, pull the "top dog" back gently and restrain him for a few seconds. Observe whether the other pup runs away and stays there, or darts back in to continue the game. Very often what we feel is unfair or overwhelming is normal play for dogs. When in doubt, "ask" the pups.

5. If you sense that play between two pups is escalating into something more serious, separate them for a few moments to cool down. If necessary, have everyone grab their pups and take a break. In fact, that would be a perfect time to have everyone practice the settle exercise.

Fearful Pups

In many puppy classes, there is at least one pup who hides behind his owners' legs, wishing to be elsewhere. This is perfectly understandable behavior in a puppy who has never been exposed to others (although the behavior also might be partially genetic). In my own classes, every one of those frightened pups improved as the class went on. In fact, some turned into real social butterflies! The trick to getting fearful pups more comfortable is two-fold: One is to let them progress at their own pace, not forcing any interactions upon them.

Make sure that none of the other pups runs at or corners them, or even interacts with them if they aren't ready. If necessary, bring a card table and stand it on its side (or create some other type of physical barrier), so the fearful dog has something to hide behind. (A barrier can also be helpful for dogs who bark incessantly at other dogs in class.)

The trickier part involves training the humans not to unwittingly reward the pup's fear. Many dog-parents, particularly those with small breeds, tend to pick their pups up and coo soothingly at the first sign of distress. The trouble is, the pups never learn to stand on their own four paws. Even those who don't pick their pups up often reward with a reinforcing, coddling tone of voice whenever the pup shows fear.

Teach your students not to coddle fearful pups. It's not that we want the puppy to be traumatized—in fact, it's just the opposite. We want the pup to see that the pack leader, the human, is obviously not worried by what's going on, so there is no need for them to be, either. There is a huge difference between saying in a sing-song, jovial voice, "Silly, that's just another dog. Go play!" (or even laying a comforting hand on the pup and saying calmly, "Youre fine,") and attempting to soothe the pup with a worried-sounding, "Oh, my poor Tootsie, did that dog scare you?" Dogs take their cues from their humans.

You may have to remind owners repeatedly during the course not to coddle. They may, however, reward their pups with soft praise for interacting properly with the other pups. Fearful pups *will* improve in your classes when allowed to move at their own pace with their owners acting appropriately. (For more on fear issues, see *Help For Your Fearful Dog* in *Resources*.)

Let's Play a Game!

Games that teach puppies and give them confidence should be played throughout Puppy Kindergarten. As mentioned, "Pass the Puppy" allows each student to handle each pup, teaches pups to accept human handling, and is invaluable for future vet and groomer visits. When the pups are passed, if they have already learned sit or down, everyone can take a turn at getting each pup to perform the skills. This often results in gales of laughter and comments such as, "Can we keep this one instead?"

Depending on the pups' comfort levels, owners could also play at petting each pup in various ways. For example, they could tug lightly at the tail or ears, or pat the pups palm-down over the head with a pat-pat-pat motion. After all, it's inevitable that a child or even an adult will approach the pup that way, and it's best for them to get used to it now. The fact that each tug or pat is followed up with a treat gets pups to actually enjoy the interactions. You will be surprised at how much fun this game is for pups and people, and will no doubt come up with your own twists on it. Just be sure you are familiar with the temperament of each pup in class before playing this game. For fearful pups, either modify the game (for example, the pup could be walked up to each person on leash, with each person feeding a treat) or do not have them participate until they feel a bit more confident.

Another fun Puppy Kindergarten activity is Dressup Day, where owners don strange-looking hats, dark sunglasses, fake noses, costumes, uniforms and anything else they'd like, and wear them for the duration of the lesson. (You could ask them to come dressed for the occasion, or have an assortment of hats, glasses, and other fun dress-up gear on hand.) Anything goes! Kids in particular really get into this game; adults love it too. The more serious purpose, of course, is that pups get familiar with these potentially scary things in a fun way. Owners could even wear the strange accessories while playing Pass the Puppy.

There is an endless variety of games that can be played in puppy class. You could place a pile of socks and T-shirts in the middle of the room, then have a race to see who can dress their pup the fastest. If you have the space, you could have owners play Hide and Seek with their pups (one at a time), each owner hiding and then calling their pup. Hide and seek is great for teaching pups to keep an eye on and check in with their owners, and is good practice for the recall.

Other Puppy K Activities

In addition to handling exercises, restraint exercises should be practiced in class. Restraint mimics what a veterinarian might do, and teaches pups to remain calm and still when necessary. Owners should be instructed not only on how to hold or restrain their pups, but to hold gently but firmly if the pup squirms, then praise gently and release when he relaxes.

Massage is another important thing to teach owners about. Daily massage is a wonderful way for owners to bond with their pups, and can alert them to any physical abnormalities they might have missed otherwise, such as cysts or tender spots.

You should also provide novel objects for pups to get used to, such as a child's expandable tunnel, a plastic ladder laid on the ground, a low A-frame, a cardboard carton to climb through, or any other "odd" things you can think of. Once pups have been introduced to each object, you could even combine the objects into a makeshift agility course. Interacting with new things boosts puppy confidence. It also gives you an opportunity to coach owners on their own reactions when their pups display fear at encountering unfamiliar objects.

Puppy Graduation

Although it's not mandatory, your Puppy Kindergarten course could culminate in a graduation ceremony. Owners are so proud of their little ones! Graduation night puts a smile on everyone's faces, and ends the course on a high note.

You could play a puppy version of the "My Dog Can Do That" card game, which is always fun. Or, you could play Musical Chairs, or have a contest to see which pup can do the most sits (or downs) in one minute. Have a contest for the longest eye contact with the owner, or something silly, like the best tail wag. Certificates and prizes should be handed out, along with a list of great dog training books, business cards and promotional fridge magnets.

At the end of puppy class, it is important to give owners information about what to do next. If you don't offer a basic obedience class, refer them to someone who does. Stress the importance of continuing to socialize the pups, and of incorporating the obedience exercises into their daily routines. Tell owners that just because their pups have become comfortable around other dogs, that does not mean they will stay that way.

A puppy who goes to class but does not get continued exposure to other dogs will, over time, become "desocialized," and all that good work will have gone to waste. Suggest that students get together with each other for play dates, as well as playing new dogs outside of those they have met in class. And give yourself a pat on the back for getting those pups and owners off to a great start!

21

Group Class Tips

Whether you are teaching classes for adult dogs or puppies, here are some helpful tips:

1. Always start on time. If your class is scheduled to begin at 7:00 p.m. and only two dog/owner teams are present at that time, begin the class anyway. If you constantly wait for stragglers, your students will realize it's okay to arrive late. If you start classes on time, students will begin to show up promptly, and even early; no one wants to miss out. It doesn't hurt, either, to randomly reward the first person to show up to class, or those who arrive promptly. Rewards can include candy (except chocolate, which is toxic to dogs), coupons that can be collected and redeemed later for prizes, clickers, or anything other small, fun, inexpensive items you can think of.

2. Owners are often nervous on the first day of class. Put them at ease by suggesting that they not compare their dog's performance to others in the class. Dogs, like people, learn at their own pace. The wonderful thing is that each dog, regardless of its ability at the start, will improve over the course of the class. It also helps to tell owners not to be embarrassed by barking or any other types of "misbehavior" their dogs display. After all, there would be no need for a class if the dogs were already perfect!

3. While certain information is crucial to impart, take care that your classes do not turn into lectures. If a subject is one that would take up a lot of class time, present it in the form of a handout instead. People only process a small percentage of information that is given in lecture form anyway, so a handout is your best bet. Keep classes moving. Explain an

exercise, demonstrate it with a student's dog (try to use each dog at least once during the course), then give feedback as the students practice. Alternate exercises with games to keep the class stimulating. If you find that students are becoming frustrated or tense during an exercise, take a brief break. Suggest that everybody stop, stretch, and take a deep breath. That will put both people and dogs at ease, and will give you the time to consider how to break the exercise into smaller, easier pieces so everyone will succeed.

4. Be as positive with the students as you are with the dogs. This is *extremely* important! Some instructors are excellent with dogs, but lack "people skills." Rather than telling a student that what he or she is doing is wrong, phrase it in a positive way, for example, "That's a good start; now try it this way..." No one wants to be told they're doing something wrong, especially in front of a group. If you must point out something that is being done incorrectly, wait until the exercise is over, then address the class as a whole: "Good job, everyone! Here are some things to watch out for..." The only reason to single someone out in front of the group is to highlight something positive. Remember, a good obedience class motivates both dogs and people, and makes them feel good about themselves. It's fun, too, to give praise and/or rewards for asking good questions, or for doing an exercise especially well.

5. Structure your classes so exercises that require more energy such as the recall are done at the beginning of class, while low-energy exercises such as stay or down are done toward the end, when the dogs are pleasantly worn out. Smart structuring is one more way to set everyone up to succeed.

6. Keep instructions and concepts simple. Analogies are helpful for getting your point across. For example, when you talk about catching dogs doing something right and rewarding the behavior, you could use this example: "Let's say every time you picked *that* chair to sit in, I ran over and gave you fifty dollars. I bet you'd soon be sitting in that chair more often! It's the same with your dog. If every time he lies calmly in his bed, you come over and give him a tummyrub, he'll be laying calmly in that bed a lot more often." Contrast that with saying, "Each time your dog presents the proper behavior, present him with positive reinforcement." Although the latter statement is correct, people will "get" the first one better.

7. Remind owners to integrate what their dogs have learned into everyday situations. Once a dog learns sit, the owner should have him sit before meals, going for walks, and anything else the dog finds rewarding. (This is good leadership practice.)

Incorporate real-life games into your classes. For example, toward the end of a seven-week adult group session, I had students play a game that incorporated leave it, sit, stay, and heel. I filled a paper grocery bag with empty egg cartons, plastic bottles and other packing, almost to the point of overflowing. A course had been prepared that contained cookies on plates, toys, and other enticements. Each owner had to weave through the course carrying the bag, dog by her side on a loose leash, telling the dog to "leave it" whenever necessary. At the end of the course was a doorway (create one by placing two chairs a few feet apart if you don't have an actual door in the area). The dog had to sit and stay while the owner fumbled in her pocket for the key, then pantomimed putting the key in the door and opening it. The game is great fun, and makes use of the skills dogs and owners have learned. Best of all, it's great practice for real-life situations.

8. Once a skill has been taught, students must help their dogs to generalize it. In other words, just because a dog understands what "sit" means, that does not mean he will do it regardless of the circumstances. For example, a dog learns that sit means to sit, facing his owner. Then, when the dog is expected to sit by his owner's side when the owner stops walking, the dog swings his rear out to the side. After all, sit means to face the owner, and the dog is trying to do just that. It is important to "change the scene" for the dog. Sit, for example, should be practiced in different positions such as facing the owner, by the owner's side, with the owner at a distance, and even with the owner sitting down. While it is important that owners practice at home with no distractions at first, encourage them to "take it on the road" by practicing in different rooms, in the back yard, front yard, outside the house, and then in various locations away from home.

9. Classes can be chaotic at times, especially if you are working with a large number of dogs. Teaching owners to reward their dogs for paying attention, particularly at the first class or two, will help immensely. If you are doing a clicker training class, have owners click and treat any

time their dogs look at them. If the class does not use clickers, have the owners say, "Yes!" each time their dogs look at them, then treat. Your classes will run much more smoothly and quietly if you can get owners to get their dogs to focus on them.

10. Point out to owners that one of the best tools they have for training their dogs is *their* behavior. Explain and demonstrate about human body language and how it affects dogs. Talk about how stress transfers down the leash, and how calm does as well. Rehearse with students what to do if their dogs become reactive with other dogs. Point out (nicely, of course!) when owners are starting to raise their voices, get tense, or otherwise influence their dogs in a negative way with their own behavior.

11. When teaching group classes, you will encounter all personality types—and I'm referring to the people, not the dogs. Some will be disruptive; some will want to tell long, involved stories about their dogs; some will ask more questions than you have time for; others will argue with just about anything you say. The books in the *Resources* section about dealing with people should be of great assistance. If someone is truly and repeatedly disruptive, speak with the person privately after class, or call during the week and try to resolve the issue.

12. While it's great fun to be the center of attention and to hear comments about how wonderful you are, *it's not about you*. A good instructor is there to support the students and their dogs, and to make *them* look good. After all, you're not the one the dogs will ultimately have to listen to. Students should think you are a good teacher, of course, but more importantly, they should come away feeling good about all they and their dogs have learned, and feeling confident that *they* are good trainers.

Endnote

Hasta La Viszla, Baby!

Well, friends, this brings us to the end of the road for now. I hope you have found the information in these pages helpful. If you visit the Phantom Publishing website (www.phantompub.com) you'll find more of my books and seminar DVDs for dog trainers, covering everything from dealing with people to working with aggression cases. But regardless of how many books you read or DVDs you watch, becoming a good trainer is a process, and this is just the beginning. Take it a step at a time, and try not to get overwhelmed. With experience will come confidence, knowledge, and success. And remember, the best trainers are the ones who never stop learning!

One last thing...the time may come when you are a well-established trainer, and a novice trainer contacts you for help. Remember what it's like to be starting out and in need of assistance. Try not to see the other trainer as potential competition—there are enough poorly behaved dogs to go around. Be generous and treat new trainers as you would like others to have treated you at the beginning. The more good, positive trainers out there, the better it will be for dogs everywhere.

Lots of luck, success, and happy, wagging tails to you!

Resources

Recommended Books/DVDs

There are many excellent books and DVDs available on training and behavior. While it would be impossible to list them all here, this collection should provide a good start to a well-rounded training education. Most are available through Dogwise (1-800-776-2665 or www.dogwise.com), amazon.com, or your local book store.

Training & Behavior

Train Your Dog: The Positive, Gentle Method (DVD)
(starring Nicole Wilde and Laura Bourhenne)
CA: The Picture Company, Inc., 2003 UPC 829637 12237 0
www.nicolewilde.com

Dog-Friendly Dog Training (2nd ed.)
Andrea Arden
New York, N.Y.: Howell Books, 1999 ISBN 9780470115145

The Culture Clash
Jean Donaldson
Oakland, CA: James & Kenneth Publishers, 1996 ISBN 1-888047-05-4

Before and After Getting Your Puppy
Ian Dunbar
Oakland, CA: James & Kenneth Publishers, 2004 ISBN 1577314557

How to Teach a New Dog Old Tricks
Ian Dunbar
Oakland, CA: James & Kenneth Publishers, 1991 ISBN 1-888047-03-8

Handbook of Applied Dog Behavior and Training
(Textbook style, information-intensive. Not "easy reading" but worth it.)
Steve Lindsay
Volume 1: Adaptation & Learning
Volume 2: Biology and Assessment of Behavior Problems
Volume 3: Procedures and Protocols
Ames, Iowa: Blackwell Publishing: available through Dogwise

How to Be the Leader of The Pack
(Dr. McConnell's booklets can be ordered in bulk at www.patriciamcconnell.com)
Patricia B. McConnell, Ph.D.
Black Earth, WI: Dog's Best Friend Ltd., 1996 ISBN 1-891767-02-X

The Power of Positive Dog Training
Pat Miller
New York: Hungry Minds, Inc., 2001 ISBN 0-7645-3609-5

Clinical Behavioral Medicine for Small Animals
(Textbook style, packed with valuable information. Includes extensive listing
of step-by-step protocols for modifying behavior issues.)
Karen L. Overall
St. Louis, Missouri: Mosby, 1997 ISBN 0-8016-6820-4

The Dog Whisperer: A Compassionate,
Non-Violent Approach to Dog Training (2nd ed.)
Paul Owens
Hollbrook, MA: Adams Media Corp., 2007 ISBN 978-1-59337-598-0

The Dog Whisperer: Beginning & Intermediate Dog Training (DVD)
Paul Owens
Sand Castle Enterprises, LLC, 2004
www.dogwhispererdvd.com, 800-955-5440

Don't Shoot the Dog (includes clicker training)
Karen Pryor
New York: Bantam Books, Inc., 1984 ISBN 0-553-25388-3

Excel-erated Learning
Pamela J. Reid, Ph.D.
Oakland, CA: James & Kenneth Publishers, 1996 ISBN 1888047070

Tawzer Dog Videos
Videos and DVDs of training and behavior seminars
888-566-3003
www.tawzerdogvideos.com

Aggression

Aggression in Dogs
Brenda Aloff
Collierville, TN: Fundcraft, Inc. ISBN 1-59196-073-8

Dogs Are From Neptune
Jean Donaldson
Quebec: Lasar Multimedia Productions Inc., 1998 ISBN 0-9684207-1-0

Fight! A Practical Guide to the Treatment of Dog-Dog Aggression
Jean Donaldson
Kinship Communications, 2004 ISBN 0-9705629-6-9

Mine! A Guide to Resource Guarding in Dogs
Jean Donaldson
Kinship Communications, 2002 ISBN 0970562942

Feisty Fido: Help for the Leash-Aggressive Dog
Patricia B. McConnell, Ph.D.
Black Earth, WI: Dog's Best Friend, Ltd., 2003

Getting a Grip on Aggression Cases
Nicole Wilde
Santa Clarita, CA: Phantom Publishing, 2008 ISBN 978-0-9817227-1-9

Body Language

Dog Language: An Encyclopedia of Canine Behavior (2nd ed.)
Roger Abrantes
Wakan Tanka Publishers, dist. by Dogwise Publishing, 1997 ISBN 0-9660484-0-7

Canine Body Language: A Photographic Guide
Brenda Aloff
Distributed by Dogwise Publishing. 2005 ISBN 1-929242-35-2

Language of Dogs (DVD)
Sarah Kalnajs
www.bluedogtraining.com/608-213-5304

The Other End of the Leash (must-read--canine/human body language)
Patricia B. McConnell, Ph.D.
NY: The Ballantine Publishing Group, 2002 ISBN 034544678X

On Talking Terms with Dogs: Calming Signals (2nd edition)
Turid Rugaas (DVD available as well)
Wenatchee, WA: Dogwise Publishing, 2006 ISBN 1929242360

Child/Dog Relations

Living with Kids and Dogs…Without Losing Your Mind
Colleen Pelar, CPDT
Woodbridge, VA: C&R Publishing, LLC, 2005 ISBN 1-933562-66-8

Raising Puppies & Kids Together: A Guide for Parents
Pia Silvani and Lynn Eckhardt
Neptune, NJ: T.F.H. Publications, 2005 ISBN 0793805686

Doggone Safe
www.doggonesafe.com (articles, Doggone Safe board game and more)

Family Paws
(Articles, educational CD, phone consults, Dogs and Storks™ program)
www.familypaws.com
919-961-1608

Fear Issues

The Cautious Canine (small, available in bulk/fear and fear-based aggression)
Patricia B. McConnell, Ph.D.
Black Earth, WI: Dog's Best Friend, Ltd., 2002 ISBN 1-891767-00-3

Help for your Fearful Dog
Nicole Wilde
Santa Clarita, CA: Phantom Publishing, 2006 ISBN 0-9667726-7-9

Separation Anxiety

Canine Separation Anxiety Workbook
James O'Heare
Ottawa, Canada: DogPsych, 2002 ISBN 0-96896668-3-7

I'll Be Home Soon (separation anxiety)
Patricia B. McConnell, Ph.D.
Black Earth, WI: Dog's Best Friend Ltd., 2000 ISBN 1-891767-05-4

Don't Leave Me! Step by Step Help for Your Dog's Separation Anxiety
Nicole Wilde
www.nicolewilde.com
Santa Clarita, CA: Phantom Publishing 2010, ISBN 978-0-0917227-3-3

Clicker Training

Click for Joy!
Melissa Alexander
Waltham, MA: Sunshine Books, 2003 ISBN 1-890948-12-8

Take A Bow Wow I & II (DVD) (trick training)
The How of Bow Wow (DVD) (obedience and other skills)
The Shape of Bow Wow - Shaping Behaviors and Adding Cues
Virginia Broitman & Sherry Lipman
Available through dogwise.com and amazon.com

Teaching Clicker Classes: Instructor's Guide
to Using Reinforcement in Dog Training
Deb Jones
Self-Published, 1996 (available through Dogwise)

Clicker Training for Dogs
Karen Pryor
Sunshine Books, 2005 ISBN 1890948217
(also see www.clickertraining.com)

Clicking with your Dog
Peggy Tillman
Waltham, MA: Sunshine Books, 2000 ISBN 1-890948-05-5

Instructing People

Dog Behavior Problems: The Counselor's Handbook
William E. Campbell
Behaviorx Systems 1999, ISBN 0966870514

The Instructor's Manual
John Rogerson
Wenatchee, WA: Direct Book Service, 1994

Coaching People to Train Their Dogs
Terry Ryan
Legacy Canine Behavior & Training, 2004 ISBN 0974246409

Teaching Dog Obedience Classes
Joachim Volhard and Gail Fisher
New York, NY: Howell Book House: 1986 ISBN 0-87605-765-2

It's Not the Dogs, It's the People!
A Dog Trainer's Guide to Training Humans
Nicole Wilde
Santa Clarita, CA: Phantom Publishing, 2003 ISBN 0-9667726-3-6

One on One: A Dog Trainer's Guide to Private Lessons
Nicole Wilde
Santa Clarita, CA: Phantom Publishing, 2004 ISBN 0-9667726-5-2

Breed Information

The Encyclopedia of the Dog
Bruce Fogle, D.V.M.
New York, NY: Dorling Kindersley, 1993 ISBN 0-7894-0149-5

Paws to Consider
Brian Kilcommons and Sarah Wilson
New York, NY: Warner Books, 1999 ISBN 0-446-52151-5

The Right Dog For You
Daniel F. Tortora, Ph.D.
New York, NY: Simon & Schuster, 1980 ISBN 0-671-47247-X

Health and Nutrition

The BARF Diet
Dr. Ian Billinghurst
Australia: Billinghurst, 2001 ISBN 0958592519

The Natural Dog: A Complete Guide For Caring Owners
Mary L. Brennan, D.V.M.
New York, NY: Penguin Books, 1993 ISBN 0-452-27019-7

Food Pets Die For: Shocking Facts about Pet Food (2nd edition)
Ann N. Martin
Troutdale, OR: NewSage Press, 2003 ISBN 0939165465

Dr. Pitcairn's Complete Guide to
Natural Health for Dogs & Cats
Pitcairn and Pitcairn
Emmaus, PA: Rodale Press, 1995 ISBN 0-87596-243-2

Natural Nutrition for Dogs and Cats (Raw foods diet)
Kymythy R. Schultze
Carlsbad, CA: Hay House, 1998 ISBN 1-56170-636-1

Natural Healing for Dogs & Cats
Diane Stein
Freedom, CA: The Crossing Press, Inc., 1993 ISBN 0-89594-686-6

Getting in Ttouch with your Dog
Linda Tellington-Jones
North Pomfret, VT: Trafalgar Square, 2001 ISBN 1570762066

The Holistic Guide for a Healthy Dog
W. Volhard & D. Brown, DVM
New York, NY: MACMILLAN, 1995 ISBN 0-87605-560-9

Miscellaneous Topics

The Dog Trainer's Resource (Vols. I & II)
(a collection of articles from the APDT Chronicle of the Dog)
Blake, Mychelle editor
Wenatchee, WA: Dogwise Publishing, 2007 ISBN 978-1-929242-39-9
Wenatchee, WA: Dogwise Publishing, 2007 ISBN 978-1-929242-57-3

Fun and Games with Dogs
Roy Hunter
United Kingdom: Howlin' Moon Press, 1995 ISBN 1888994002

Games People Play To Train Their Dogs (great game ideas for classes)
and *Life Beyond Block Heeling* (volume two of the above)
Terry Ryan
WA: Legacy By Mail, 1996

Coercion and its Fallout (Effects of the use of force on people and animals)
Murray Sidman
Boston, MA: Authors Cooperative, Inc., 1989 ISBN 0962331112

How To Market Your Dog Training Business
Lisa K. Wilson
CA: The Dog Trainers Marketing Resource Center, 1997

Other Publications

The Clicker Journal
www.clickertrain.com/journal.html

Patricia McConnell's books and booklets
www.patriciamcconnell.com

Sue Sternberg's booklets and videos
(Temperament testing, defensive handling, aggression and more)
Rondout Valley Kennels
4628 Route 209
Accord, NY 12404
914-687-4406
www.suesternberg.com

The Whole Dog Journal
www.whole-dog-journal.com
Subscriptions 1-800-829-9165
Back issues 1-800-424-7887

Nicole Wilde's books and DVDs
www.phantompub.com

Organizations & Education

ABTA (Animal Behavior and Training Associates)
1-800-795-3294

American College of Applied Science (ACAS)
800-403-3347
www.amcollege.com

Animal Behavior College (ABC)
800-795-3294
www.animalbehaviorcollege.com

Association of Pet Dog Trainers (APDT)
1-800-PET-DOGS
www.apdt.com

Companion Animal Sciences Institute
www.casinstitute.com

Dog Seminars Directory
www.dogseminarsdirectory.com

Dogs of Course
www.dogsofcourse.com

Flying Dog Press (Suzanne Clothier)
(upstate NY)
www.flyingdogpress.com

International Association of Animal Behavior Consultants (IAABC)
www.iaabc.org

Legacy Canine Behavior and Training (Terry Ryan)
(Sequim, WA)
888-683-1522
www.legacycanine.com

Marin Humane Society (Trish King)
(northern CA)
415-883-4621
www.marinhumanesociety.org

Moorpark College
(southern CA)
805-378-1400
www.moorpark.cc.ca.us

National Association of Dog Obedience Instructors (NADOI)
www.nadoi.org

Peacable Paws (Pat Miller)
(Maryland)
www.peaceablepaws.com

Raising Canine Telecourses
www.raisingcanine.com/coursespage.htm

San Fransisco SPCA Academy For Dog Trainers
(415) 554-3095
www.sfspca.org/academy

Sue Sternberg
(Accord, NY)
www.suesternberg.com

Certification

Certification Council for Pet Dog Trainers (CCPDT)
212-356-0682
www.cppdt.org

Products

Assess-A-Hand
Rondout Valley Kennels
4628 Route 209
Accord, NY 12404
845-687-7619
www.suesternberg.com

Clickers, Target Sticks, Bait Bags & More
www.dogwise.com, legacycanine.com, sitstay.com

Gentle Leaders, Easy Walk Harnesses and more
Premier Pet Products
www.premier.com
1-800-933-5595

KISS Manufacturing
(Promotional products including fridge magnets)
1-800-262-2868
www.kissmfg.com

Kong Company
303-216-2626
www.kongcompany.com

My Dog Can Do That!
Board game, great for graduation class, available through Dogwise.

Tethers
www.dogwhispererdvd.com/products.htm
www.pettethers.com or ph: 866-LUVADOG

Online Information

Clicker Solutions Training Treasures
Posts and articles available through www.clickersolutions.com

Dog Owner's Guide
Articles on training, breed profiles, and more.
www.canismajor.com/dog

Dog Star Daily
Blog site with a fresh variety of wonderful topics and contributors
www.dogstardaily.com

DVM Newsmagazine online
veterinarynews.dvm360.com
training & behavior articles including those by Karen Overall

Flying Dog Press
Free, online articles by Suzanne Clothier on training and behavior.
www.flyingdogpress.com

The Well Mannered Dog
Shirley Chong's Keeper Pages - a collection of training articles and posts focusing on clicker training.
www.shirleychong.com/keepers/index.html

Internet Resources

There are countless discussion lists and websites concerning dog behavior and training. These are just a few:

APDT-L (open to APDT members only)
http://groups.yahoo.com/group/apdtlist

Clicker Solutions
www.clickersolutions.com

Dog-T-Biz (focus is on business aspects of the profession)
http://finance.groups.yahoo.com/group/Dog-T-Biz

Shelter Trainers List
http://groups.yahoo.com/group/sheltertrainers

Insurance

Liability Insurance For Dog Trainers:

Business Insurers of the Carolinas
(Offers insurance specifically to APDT members)
1-800-962-4611

The Hartford Insurance Co.
1-888-253-4940

Books and DVDs for Trainers by Nicole Wilde